# The Essentials Reader

## Readings to Accompany Logic of English® Essentials 1-30

Kimber Iverson

LogicofEnglish

*The Essentials Reader: Readings to Accompany Logic of English Essentials 1-30*

Printed in the United States of America

Logic of English® is a Registered Trademark of Logic of English, Inc
Registered in the U. S. Patent and Trademark Office

Logic of English, Inc
4865 19th Street NW, Suite 130
Rochester, MN 55901


ISBN 978-1-936706-93-8

10   9   8   7   6

www.logicofenglish.com

# Table of Contents

*For the Word Fighters*

*Letters and sounds, running together*
*Pressed into words, each fought for, won*
*Sentences coaxed, paragraphs forged*
*An idea, a story, dug out of the shapes*

*Keep fighting, my friend, keep fighting for words*
*Don't ever give up or let go of your grit*
*You work so hard, I know, but someday*
*The most beautiful story you find will be yours*

*- KI*

# Unit 1

| | |
|---|---|
| quips | <u>qu</u>ips |
| grins | grins² |
| grumps | grumps |
| blends | blends² |
| pink | pink |
| blobs | blobs² |
| best | best |
| brisk | brisk |
| drops | drops |
| damp | damp |
| drum | drum |
| drinks | drinks |
| stinks | stinks |
| stunt | stunt |

# Ten Quips

Glad Gwen grins at grumps.

Brad blends pink blobs best.

Kit skips in brisk wind.

Dan drops his damp drum on his desk.

Glen left his lamp and lost his list.

Fran flips fat frogs fast.

Ted gets rest in bed.

Kris drinks pink ink. It stinks!

Stunt man Stan slips and spins on his spit.

Tom trips on ten traps.

# Unit 2

| | |
|---|---|
| that | t͟hat [2] |
| thick | t͟hi͟ck |
| tree | tr͟ee |
| thinks | t͟hinks |
| stuck | stu͟ck |
| this | t͟his [2] |
| strength | stre͟ngth |
| luck | lu͟ck |
| creep | cr͟ee͟p |
| free | fr͟ee |
| seems | s͟ee͟ms [2] |
| then | t͟hen [2] |

# Buck Got Stuck

Illustrated by Libby Johnson

Buck sees that cat in that big, thick tree
and thinks that cat is stuck.
This man can run and help that cat,
with his strength and luck!

Buck can creep up in that tree;
this man can get it free.
But then it seems this man got stuck.
That cat must then help Buck!

| | |
|---|---|
| acorns | ā c<u>or</u>ns [2] |
| Peter | Pē <u>t</u>er |
| summer | sum m<u>er</u> |
| north | <u>north</u> |
| forest | <u>for</u> est |
| hunting | hunt <u>ing</u> |
| clever | clev <u>er</u> |
| super | sū p<u>er</u> |
| hidden | hid den |
| dashes | da<u>sh</u> es [2] |
| over | ō v<u>er</u> |
| secret | sē cret |
| splendid | splen did |
| vanish | van <u>ish</u> |

# Acorns for Peter

It is summer in Big North Forest. Peter is on an acorn hunt. For him, acorn hunting is great sport. He is quick and **clever**, and it is super fun.

Peter sees acorns hidden in green grass. He dashes over to get them. He grabs them and sticks them in his secret **stash**.

Peter spots acorns on twigs. He sneaks up trees to get them. He grabs them and sticks them under rocks.

After winter has begun, he will feast on his **splendid** treats. But Peter must be quick, for winter is near and then acorns will **vanish**!

# Unit 4

| | |
|---|---|
| racing | rā cing [2] |
| team | team |
| members | mem bers [2] |
| event | ē vent |
| push | püsh |
| steer | steer |
| contact | con tact |
| person | per son |
| riding | rī ding |
| finishing | fin ish ing |
| fastest | fast est |
| wins | wins [2] |
| medal | med al |

# Bed Racing

by Christy Jones

BluIz60 / Shutterstock.com

**B**ed racing is an odd but fun sport. Bed racing is a team sport with three to seven members on a team. The team members dress up the bed and the team for the event. A team member must sit on the bed. The rest push and steer the bed.

All team members must keep in contact with the bed. Bed racing can be on a street or on a river. At river events, the person riding the bed must not fall in the river.

Teams get points for finishing the fastest and for dressing up the bed. The team that finishes the fastest wins the Fastest Bed Medal. The team that dresses up the best wins the Best Bed Medal.

BluIz60 / Shutterstock.com

| | |
|---|---|
| wombat | wom bat |
| animal | an i mal |
| ears | e̲a̲rs² |
| digesting | dī ge²st i̲n̲g |
| tunnels | tun nels² |
| protected | prō tec ted |
| enemy | en em y⁴ |
| away | ā wa̲y̲ |
| meters | mē te̲rs² |
| seconds | sec onds² |
| Olympic | Ō ly̆m pic |
| sprinter | sprin te̲r |
| brutal | brū tal |
| remember | rē mem be̲r |

# Wombats

A wombat is a funny animal. It has a thick body with short legs. A wombat has a very short tail. It has a big head with small ears, and it has big, strong teeth. A wombat eats grass and shrubs. Then it spends up to 2 weeks digesting its meal!

Wombats dig many tunnels. A tunnel can be up to 30 meters long. That is as long as three buses!

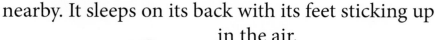

A wombat sleeps in the day. It sleeps in its tunnel or nearby. It sleeps on its back with its feet sticking up in the air.

A wombat mom has a pocket for its baby. But the pocket opens in the back! That is so the baby is kept clean and protected as the mom digs tunnels.

If an enemy runs after a wombat, the wombat can sprint away. A wombat can run 100 meters in less than 10

seconds. This is as fast as an Olympic sprinter! The wombat runs to its tunnel. Then the wombat blocks the enemy with its rump. If the enemy still gets into the tunnel, the wombat's strong back legs can kick it or even crush its head into the wall.

A wombat can be a brutal attacker. So remember, never get into combat with a wombat!

# Unit 6

| | |
|---|---|
| futnet | füt net |
| football | f<u>oo</u>t bäll [2] |
| tennis | ten nis |
| invented | in ven ted |
| soccer | soc c<u>er</u> |
| similar | sim i l<u>ar</u> |
| across | ā cross |
| any | an y [4] |
| except | ex cept [2] |
| opponent | op pō nent |
| increasingly | in cr<u>ea</u>s <u>in</u>g ly [4] |
| popular | pop ū l<u>ar</u> |
| global | glō bal |

# Futnet

Futnet, or football tennis, was invented in 1922. It is a blend of soccer and tennis. Each team has up to three players. The ball is similar to a soccer ball. The net is 1.1 meters tall and 9 meters across. To get points, players must hit the ball over the net with any part of the body except the hands or arms.

A good player can run fast and kick the ball far up in the air. A good player can jump up in the air and smash the ball over the net so his **opponent** cannot reach it. A great player can even hit it off his head, or land on a hand to reach the ball with his foot.

Futnet has lots of kicking, running, jumping, and twisting. Today futnet is an increasingly popular, **global** sport.

Source: EFTA

# Unit 7

| | |
|---|---|
| call | cäll |
| Shelly | Shel ly⁴ |
| yippee | yip pee |
| freedom | free dom |
| woohoo | woo hoo |
| focus | fō cus |
| ready | rēad² y⁴ |
| toiling | toil ing |
| groaning | groan ing |
| coax | coax |
| mother | moth² er |
| happy | hap py⁴ |
| attempts | at tempts |
| dismay | dis may |

# Just Call Her Shelly

"**Y**ippee! It is Freedom Day!"

The duckling has waited so long for this day – the day of the Big Push, the Break-Away, a fresh breath of air, the freedom to spread her wings!

But she cannot enjoy this day until she gets her shell off.

She pecks and pecks until her head gets free.

"Woohoo! Look at me! Smell this fresh air!"

"Oops!" The shell tips and teeters. She **reels over**.

"Focus!" she thinks.

Then she digs and digs with her toes. The shell cracks. Her feet push free.

She rocks up onto her feet. She stops to rest and mops away her sweat.

"Ready? Go!" she tells herself.

She strains and presses over and over. **Toiling** and groaning, she pushes at her shell. But she cannot **coax** that shell apart!

"Arg!" she moans.

"Let me free!" she wails.

Just then Mother Duck hops along. She is happy to see her baby duckling.

Then her mother sees the problem.

She attempts to help her duckling. But to her **dismay**, the shell will not crack. The shell will not break. The shell is stuck!

Mother pats her duckling on the head and tells her, "That is okay, dear, it is a great shell. Just keep it on."

Even today, the duckling still wears that shell as if it is a dress. And that is the reason her mother calls her "Shelly."

# Unit 8

| | |
|---|---|
| weather | wea̲t̲h̲ er̲ |
| different | dif fe̲r ent |
| result | rē sult |
| humidity | hū mid i ty |
| lighter | li̲g̲h̲t er̲ |
| begins | bē gins |
| retains | rē ta̲i̲ns |
| lightning | li̲g̲h̲t ni̲n̲g̲ |
| tornadoes | to̲r nā dō̲e̲s |
| whether | w̲h̲e̲t̲h̲ er̲ |
| whatever | w̲h̲ät ev er̲ |
| experiment | ex per i ment |
| coloring | col o̲r ing |

# Weather

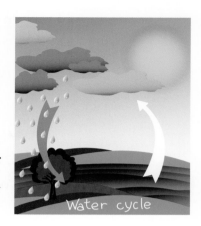

Water cycle

**D**ifferent weather happens when air shifts. Shifting air is the result of different levels of heat and **humidity**. Humidity is water in the air.

Warm air is lighter than cool air. When warm air and cool air meet, the cool air sinks and pushes under the warm air. The cool air lifts warmer air up.

On sunny days the sun heats up the land. Then the land warms the air near it. The air near the land gets warmer than the air up high. When this happens, the warm air lifts up higher. As it lifts, it cools. Then the high, cool air sinks. As it sinks near the land, it warms up again. Then the shifting begins all over.

On warm days the sun also heats up the sea. When air is near water, the air gets warm and humid. Warm air **retains** water better than cool air. When the warm, humid air lifts up high, it cools off. As it cools it lets go of the water. This results in rain.

When cool air, warm air, and humid air shift, it can result in wind, storms, thunder, lightning, hail, and even tornadoes.

# Whether the Weather

adapted from an anonymous poem

**W**hether the weather is fair,
or whether the weather is not;
Whether the weather is cool,
or whether the weather is hot;
We must weather the weather,
whatever the weather,
whether we want to or not.

# A Weather Experiment

**D**o this experiment to see the effect of heat:
1. Fill a clear glass with cool water.
2. Fill a second clear glass with cool water.
3. Add three drops of food coloring to the second glass.
4. Add the water with food coloring to the glass of water with no food coloring. What happens?
5. Then fill a clear glass with hot water.
6. Fill another glass with cool water.
7. Put three drops of food coloring into the cool water.
8. Add the cool water to the hot water. What happens? Is it different?

# Unit 9

| | |
|---|---|
| astronaut | as trō n<u>au</u>t |
| experiments | ex per i ments |
| planets | plan ets |
| solar system | sō l<u>ar</u> sў̆s tem |
| equipment | ē <u>qu</u>ip ment |
| robotic | rō bot ic |
| beginning | bē gin ni<u>ng</u> |
| dizzy | diz zy[4] |
| gravity | grav i ty[4] |
| differently | dif f<u>er</u> ent ly[4] |
| easy | <u>eas</u>[2] y[4] |
| utensils | ū ten sils[2] |
| liquids | li <u>qu</u>ids[2] |

# Astronauts

Being an astronaut is a demanding job. Each astronaut **aboard** a flight must do tasks each day. Astronauts conduct lots of experiments. The experiments help them to understand the planets, the sun, and the solar system. Astronauts repair equipment. An astronaut can also run a **robotic** arm to fix things on the shell of the ship.

Astronaut living can be difficult. In the beginning, astronauts may feel dizzy or sick. With no **gravity**, everything can float, so astronauts must do things differently. It is easy to lift things, but it

An astronaut on the job

NASA

NASA

Astronauts eating floating food for lunch

can be hard to keep things from floating away.

To eat dinner, an astronaut might need to add water to food packets and heat them. **Utensils** such as forks and spoons can attach to a food tray with Velcro™ to keep them near. Even liquids can float away, so the astronauts drink from bags with straws.

Sleep is a bit different too. Instead of sleeping in normal beds, astronauts sleep in sleeping bags with seat belts that strap them to a wall and keep them from drifting away in the night. Astronauts must do lots of things differently!

# Unit 10

| | |
|---|---|
| molasses | mō las seš [2] |
| banana | ban an ä |
| coffee | cof <u>fee</u> |
| preheat | prē h<u>ea</u>t |
| oven | ov en |
| another | an o<u>th</u>[2] er |
| batter | bat t<u>er</u> |
| hour | <u>hour</u> |
| toothpick | t<u>oo</u>th pick |
| center | cen[2] t<u>er</u> |
| ready | r<u>ea</u>[2]d y[4] |

# Molasses Banana Bread

This dark brown bread is sweet, but not too sweet. It is great with a meal or as a snack with coffee, tea, or milk.

1/2 cup soft butter
1 egg
1/2 cup molasses
4 bananas
2 cups wheat flour
1/2 teaspoon baking soda
1/2 teaspoon baking powder
1/2 teaspoon salt
1/2 teaspoon ground nutmeg
Oil or melted butter for the pan

**Preheat** the oven to 350°F. Coat a bread pan with the oil or melted butter. Mash the bananas until no lumps remain. In a big bowl, **cream** the butter with a spoon or mixer. Add the egg, molasses, and bananas and beat well. In another bowl, mix together the flour, baking soda, baking powder, salt, and nutmeg. Then add them to the big bowl and mix. Pour the batter into the pan. Put it in the oven and cook it for about an hour until it is a bit darker on top. Test it by sticking a toothpick in the center of the loaf. If it is clean when you pull it out, the bread is ready. Let it cool, then enjoy it!

| | |
|---|---|
| Felix | Fē lix |
| every | ev <u>er</u> y [4] |
| around | ā <u>rou</u>nd |
| laughs | <u>lau</u><u>gh</u>s [2] |
| nobody | nō bod y [4] |
| talk | tä<u>l</u>k |
| you | y<u>ou</u> [3] |
| sullen | sul len |
| grandfather | grand fä<u>th</u> <u>er</u> [2] |
| dejected | dē jec ted |
| cousin | c<u>ou</u> sin [4] [2] |
| disgusting | dis gust <u>ing</u> |
| wounded | w<u>ou</u>n ded [3] |
| ordeal | <u>or</u> d<u>ea</u>l |

# Felix the Frog

Felix the Frog is good at catching bugs. He can catch them hopping forward, and he can catch them hopping backward. He can catch them as he jumps up, and he can catch them as he lands back down. He can catch black bugs and green bugs and brown bugs. He can catch every bug in the pond.

On a bright, sunny day, Felix sees a different sort of bug. It is big and red. It buzzes around his head. Felix smacks his lips, leaps up, and attempts to catch it. But the red bug is too fast. It laughs as it gets away, saying, "Ha! Ha! Ha! Nobody can eat me!"

Felix hops after the bug. He attempts another catch, and another, and another. But each attempt fails. The red bug laughs, saying, "Ha! Ha! Ha! Nobody can eat me!"
Felix hops away, feeling sad and upset.

He hops over to talk to Mother Frog. "I can catch black bugs. I can catch green bugs. I can catch brown bugs. But I cannot catch that big, fast, red bug! How can I

catch it?"

Mother Frog looks at him and tells him, "You must leap higher. Then you will catch it."

So Felix hops back to the pond and waits for the red bug to buzz around again. When it gets near him, he leaps up as high as he can

and attempts to catch it. But the bug laughs and gets away, saying, "Ha! Ha! Ha! Nobody can eat me!" Felix hops away, feeling **sullen** and **cross**.

He hops over to talk to Grandfather Frog. "I can catch black bugs. I can catch green bugs. I can catch brown bugs. But I cannot catch that big, fast, red bug! How can I catch that bug?"

Grandfather Frog looks at him and tells him, "You must sit on that big rock at the other end of the pond. Then you will catch it."

So Felix hops across the pond, leaps up on the rock, and sits down to wait for the bug. When it gets near him, he leaps up off the rock and attempts to catch it. But the bug laughs and gets away, saying, "Ha! Ha! Ha! Nobody can eat me!" Felix hops away, feeling angry and **dejected**.

He hops over to talk to Cousin Toad. "I can

catch black bugs. I can catch green bugs. I can catch brown bugs. But I cannot catch that big, fast, red bug! How can I catch that bug?"

Cousin Toad looks at him and tells him, "You must pretend to be asleep. Then you will catch it."

So Felix hops back to the pond. He pretends to be asleep. Just as the bug buzzes near his head, he suddenly leaps up and... he catches it! But the second he gets it in his mouth, he spits it out again. "Yuck! What a disgusting bug!" He keeps spitting and spitting, but he cannot get the bad flavor out of his mouth.

The big red bug, however, is not even wounded from the **ordeal**! He laughs and zooms away, saying, "Ha! Ha! Ha! Nobody can eat me!"

| | |
|---|---|
| known | kn<u>ow</u>n² |
| kinds | kīnds² |
| many | man y⁴ |
| shallow | sh<u>a</u>l l<u>ow</u>² |
| tropics | trop ics |
| polar | pō l<u>ar</u> |
| centimeter | cen ti mē t<u>er</u>² |
| opening | ō pen <u>ing</u> |
| goes | g<u>ōe</u>s² |
| through | <u>thr</u><u>ough</u>³ |
| stomach | stom a<u>ch</u>² |
| predators | pred ā t<u>ors</u>² |
| poison | p<u>oi</u>² son |
| millions | mil⁴ l<u>i</u>ons² |

# Stars of the Sea

Over 1,500 known kinds of starfish, or sea stars, can be found on the floor of the sea. Many starfish **dwell** in warm, shallow water in the **tropics**. But starfish also exist in cold **polar** areas and as deep as 6,000 meters under the sea!

Starfish can be as small as 1 centimeter or as big as 1 meter. Lots of starfish look bright and colorful. But others blend into the background to keep from being seen.

It is common to think of starfish with 5 arms, but starfish can be found with 6 or 10 or even 50 arms! Each arm has small feet that can grip things or help the starfish get around. A starfish can even see with a spot on the tip of each of its arms!

BELOW: This starfish sees with the red spot on the tip of its arm. The small feet help it get around.

André-Philipe D. Picard / Wikipedia.com

BELOW:
Crown-of-thorns
Starfish.

On the top of a starfish, a small opening lets seawater in or out. This helps the starfish crawl, cling to things, eat, and get air. The water goes in the opening on top. Then the water goes through the starfish and out its feet!

Starfish eat small sea animals such as clams, oysters, and snails. The mouth is under the starfish in the center. If a starfish wants to eat, it crawls on top of its food. Then the starfish sucks the food into its stomach. Or it might push its stomach out of its body to **engulf** the food! A starfish can pull apart a clamshell with its arms. It then inserts its stomach into the shell to eat the clam meat! After it eats the food, it brings its stomach back into its body.

A number of other animals eat starfish, such as otters, seagulls, crabs, big snails, and even other starfish. Different kinds of starfish do different things to keep **predators** away. A starfish might protect itself with sharp thorns all over its body. Another might **emit** poison into the water. Or a starfish may send a warning sign to predators by changing its color.

If a predator grabs the arm of a starfish, the starfish might shed the arm so it can get away! Later, it can grow another arm. In fact, many kinds of starfish can grow another body just from the arm!

Starfish lay millions of eggs each year. When an egg hatches, it floats near the top of the water. It grows into an adult in 2-5 years, depending on which kind of starfish it is. A starfish can get to be 5, 10, or even 35 years old! That is old for a starfish!

BELOW: This starfish is growing another arm.

# Unit 13

| very | vĕr y⁴ |
| family | fam i ly⁴ |
| lazy | lā zy⁴ |
| several | sev <u>er</u> al |
| every | ev <u>er</u> y⁴ |
| disgusting | dis gust <u>ing</u> |
| soundly | s<u>ou</u>nd ly⁴ |
| clamor | clam <u>or</u> |
| swords | s<u>w</u><u>or</u>²ds |
| enough | ē n<u>ough</u>⁵ |
| laugh | <u>laugh</u>² |
| sorry | sor ry⁴ |
| tormented | t<u>or</u> ment ed |

# The Toothpick Fighters

Adapted from a Traditional Japanese Folktale
Illustrated by Libby Johnson

Long ago in Japan, it was common to cover the floors with thick, soft mats of woven **reeds**. The mats had to be kept very clean, for the family sat, slept, and even had meals on the floor. The family did not wear shoes indoors, and children had to learn never to harm the mats or get dirt on them.

Most children in Japan did a great job of being neat and clean. But now and then a child did not do such a good job. In fact, in a small fishing town on the coast was a girl who had a bad **habit**. At night when she went to bed, she always wanted to pick her teeth with a toothpick.

Now, it was not so bad that she wanted to pick her teeth with a toothpick. The bad part was that after she did it, she was too lazy to get up out of bed to throw it away. Instead, she stuck the toothpick between the reeds of the mat near her bed.

After several months, the mat was so full of

toothpicks that every crack had toothpicks stuck in it. This was not a clean habit at all! Every toothpick was dirty with bits of food stuck to it! Disgusting!

This went on and on until a very odd night. The girl was sleeping soundly when all of a sudden she was woken up by a loud **clamor**.

When she took a look, she saw lots of small men, each about three inches high. Each man had a teeny sword and was fighting another  man. The shouting, grunting, and clashing of swords was shocking.

At first she thought it was a dream. But when she bit her lip, it hurt. This had to be real! She was so afraid, she did not sleep for the rest of the night.

The next night, she was woken up again by the loud **rumpus**. Again she was so afraid that she did not go back to sleep. Night after night, this kept happening. And night after night, she did not get enough sleep.

Soon the girl was so sleepy that she started feeling sick. Her father saw her looking sad and **frail**. He wanted to know what the problem was. But she did not want to tell him what was happening. She thought he might laugh at her. He kept asking, though, so at last she told him.

Her father did not laugh, but he also did not trust her. He wanted to see the men for himself. So he thought of a plan.

That night, he kept watch over his daughter through a crack in the door. At midnight he saw the small men enter. He saw them pick up toothpicks to fight each other. He saw them grinning and having fun. All that fighting was really just playing!

The men acted so funny with the teeny toothpick swords. He just wanted to laugh! But then he saw his daughter was afraid. Instead of  laughing, he took out his big sword. He burst into the room. The small men suddenly let go of the teeny swords and ran away. All that was left was a mess of toothpicks.

The father told his daughter that the toothpicks had attracted the small men. The men thought it was so much fun to turn the toothpicks into swords and pretend to fight each other.

"But how did the toothpicks get into the mat?" he wanted to know.

The girl was **reluctant** to admit her bad habit. But at last she told him that she had felt too lazy to get up and throw away her toothpicks, and had stuck them in the mat instead. She told her father she was sorry. Then the girl collected all the toothpicks, even the toothpicks that had fallen into the cracks, and put them in the trash.

The next night, with no toothpicks to fight with, the toothpick fighters did not return. She was never **tormented** by them again. At last she started to sleep well at night, and soon she was feeling much better. The girl never forgot the toothpick fighters though, and from then on, she always got rid of her toothpicks properly.

# Unit 14

| | |
|---|---|
| William | Wil liäm[4] |
| Kamkwamba | Käm kwäm bä |
| Malawi | Mä lä wi[3] |
| community | com mū ni ty[4] |
| uniform | ū ni <u>form</u> |
| learning | <u>lear</u> ni<u>ng</u> |
| engineer | en gin[2] <u>eer</u> |
| scorched | sc<u>orch</u>ed[3] |
| drought | dr<u>ough</u>t[4] |
| throughout | <u>through</u> <u>out</u>[3] |
| hungry | hun gry[4] |
| destroyed | dē str<u>oy</u>ed[2] |
| library | lī brā ry[4] |
| electricity | ē lec tri ci[2] ty[4] |

# William Kamkwamba

William Kamkwamba was born on a farm in **Malawi** in 1987. With others in his community, his family grew corn. The corn was ground into cornmeal and eaten for every meal. The corn crop depended on the weather. As long as the rain fell, the corn grew and the family had food to eat.

William helped his family on the farm. He dug up the soil to get it ready for planting. He planted the seeds and tended the growing seedlings. He pulled out weeds and helped harvest the crop.

William also went to school. In Malawi, school was not free. William's family had to pay school fees. The family also had to pay for books and a school uniform. William loved learning, and he

Good corn harvest

dreamed about becoming an engineer. Although his family was poor, if the rain fell each year his family had enough food. And if the crops grew well, his father sold them to pay for school.

But in 2001, when William was 14 years old, the rain did not fall for months and months. When the rain finally did fall, it rained too hard and washed away the seeds. The ground flooded. After the floods, the rain did not fall again. The few plants that did grow got **scorched** in the sun and wilted away. The **drought**

Corn scorched in the sun

affected farms throughout Malawi. Without the corn crop, everybody was hungry. Many went to other towns to look for food, but it was hard to find any. Many began starving.

At school, William and the other children felt so hungry that it was hard to think and learn. Also, without a corn crop, his family had no way to pay his school fees. William had to drop out of school. He attempted to sneak into school for free, but then the teacher found out that he had not paid, so he had to stop. His dream of becoming an engineer was destroyed.

At first, William spent his days searching for

Schoolroom in Malawi

food, but he did not find any. He attempted to catch birds, but the birds flew away too quickly. He was always hungry, but he had no way to fill his stomach. He wanted to get his mind off his hunger.

Then he remembered the library in town. William began to visit the library often. He planned to keep up in his school subjects and to return to school when the drought was over.

He read books about all sorts of subjects, but he was most interested in engineering and electricity. When he found a book about windmills, a new dream grew in his mind. He wanted to construct a windmill to power a water pump for watering the corn. A windmill with a water pump can bring water to crops even if no rain falls. For William, a windmill meant electricity and freedom from drought and hunger.

William knew it was a big, difficult project. So first he constructed a small model of a windmill using scraps he found. He learned from his model. The small windmill generated enough electricity to power a small radio.

William's first big windmill
Tom Rielly / flickr.com

After that, William felt ready to construct a bigger windmill. A bigger windmill needed bigger parts. He found many parts at a junkyard that had lots of old cars and tractors. A good pal also bought parts for him.

When he was at the junkyard, boys from school teased him for digging in the trash. Others in town thought he was crazy. Even his mother did not understand what he was doing. But at last his big windmill was finished.

This windmill was still not big enough to power a water pump. But William hoped it was big enough to power a light bulb. When William was ready to connect the windmill to a light bulb, a crowd gathered to watch. The crowd expected it to fail. But it did not fail! It lit the light bulb! The crowd was thrilled. Everybody started calling the windmill "electric wind." And instead of calling William crazy, everybody called William smart.

William speaking to others about his windmill.
Erik (HASH) Hersman / flickr.com

Men from other towns heard about William's windmill and visited him. Reporters wanted to report about it in newspapers. Then a man who heard about William's windmill volunteered to pay his school fees. William went back to school.

William was happy. When he was not in school, he kept toiling on a new windmill. At last, William constructed a windmill that was big enough to send power to a water pump for the family farm.

Later William constructed an even bigger water pump. This water pump used **solar power**, or power from the sun, to get electricity. It was big enough to pump water to everybody in his town! William was happy that everybody in his town had enough water.

# Unit 15

| | |
|---|---|
| geothermal | gē ō ther mal |
| energy | en er gy |
| offices | of fi ces |
| fossil fuels | fos sil fū els |
| poisonous | poi son ous |
| chemicals | chem i cals |
| sources | sour ces |
| continuous | con tin ū ous |
| supply | sup plȳ |
| absorbs | ab sorbs |
| process | proc ess |
| system | sўs tem |
| costly | cost ly |
| develop | dē vel op |

# Geothermal Energy

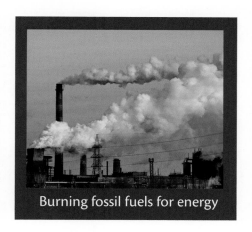

Burning fossil fuels for energy

**H**umans need energy to keep houses, offices, and schools warm in the winter and cool in the summer. We get most of the energy for heating and cooling from burning **fossil fuels**: oil, gas, and coal.

Fossil fuels, however, cannot be **renewed**. Burning fossil fuels **emits** poisonous chemicals that can harm plants, animals, and humans. Research also shows that burning fossil fuels adds to global warming.

With all the problems from burning fossil fuels, it is important to invest in other sources of energy for heating and cooling. Wind energy from windmills and solar power from the sun can be good. But wind and solar power need just the

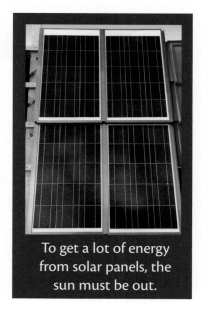

To get a lot of energy from solar panels, the sun must be out.

right weather. Geothermal energy is from the earth. It is a continuous supply of energy.

## What is geothermal energy?

The center of the Earth is melted rock that is

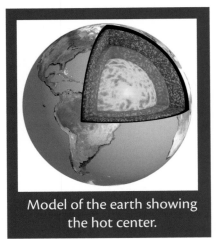

Model of the earth showing the hot center.

12,600°F. This is even hotter than the outer part of the sun! The heat in the center of the earth warms up the layers of earth farther away. Though the earth near the top is not as hot, it still **retains** much of the heat. Geothermal energy is energy **obtained** from that heat in the ground.

## Geothermal water

Water that soaks deep into the ground from rain or melted snow is called **groundwater**. The heat from the center of the Earth can warm groundwater. It can be as hot as 700°F. This hot water is called **geothermal water**.

Swimming in a hot spring heated by geothermal energy.

Water heated with geothermal heat is shooting out of the ground.

When geothermal water travels up to the top of the ground through an opening it can form pools called hot springs. Hot springs can be fun for relaxing and swimming. In a few areas, geothermal water gets so hot that water shoots up out of the ground into the air!

In many places, hot geothermal water is not too far underground. This hot water can be pumped up to heat houses, schools, and offices. It is pumped up out of the ground through a **duct**. The hot water is then sent through the walls and floors. The hot water heats the indoor air. After the geothermal water releases its heat, the cool water is pumped back into the ground to warm up again from the Earth's heat.

Geothermal water is pumped in ducts out of the ground and under the floors to heat rooms. As the water cools, it is pumped back down into the earth to warm back up.

Geothermal greenhouses for growing food in the Netherlands.

In the winter, many greenhouses get heat from geothermal water to warm the air for the plants. A few towns even put geothermal heat under streets and walkways to melt the snow in the winter!

## Geothermal heat pumps

Geothermal water, however, is not under all parts of the earth. Another way to get energy from the earth's heat is with **geothermal heat pumps**. About 20 feet under the ground, it is always about 55°F. This is partly from geothermal heat, but it is also from the heat that the land **absorbs** from the sun.

Houses with geothermal heat pumps can get this heat to keep warm in the winter. A liquid is pumped through a duct into the ground. The liquid absorbs heat from the ground and gets warmer. Then the warm liquid is pumped up through the floors and walls. In the process, the liquid emits heat into the rooms. When it has cooled, the liquid is pumped back down into the earth to warm up again. This is called a **ground loop system**.

Geothermal energy is clean, easy to get in many areas, and an important part of meeting our energy needs. Even though geothermal energy is cheaper than energy from fossil fuels, geothermal systems can still be costly to install.

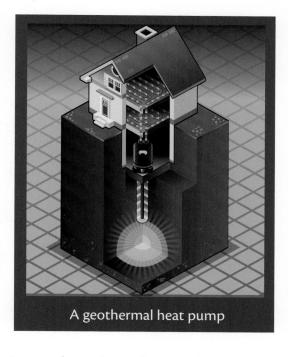

A geothermal heat pump

We need to keep learning about geothermal energy, invent better tools for digging, and develop cheaper geothermal systems.

| | |
|---|---|
| lumberjack | lum b<u>er</u> ja<u>ck</u> |
| Minnesota | Min nē sō tä |
| heavy | h<u>ea</u>v²  y⁴ |
| Arizona | Ā ri zō nä |
| before | bē fōr<u>e</u> |
| Oregon | <u>Or</u> ē gon |
| humongous | hū mon g<u>ou</u>s⁴ |
| breakfast | br<u>ea</u>²k fast |
| folks | fō<u>l</u>ks |
| everything | ev <u>er</u> y⁴ <u>thing</u> |
| everybody | ev <u>er</u> y⁴ bod y⁴ |
| thawed | <u>thawe</u>²d |
| smoothed | sm<u>oo</u>²<u>the</u>²d |
| California | Cal i <u>for</u> niä⁴ |

# The Tale of Paul Bunyan

So did you ever hear about that lumberjack with the name of Paul Bunyan? Well, let me tell you. He was so tall, his head was higher than the treetops! That's right, he was that tall.

It's **hard to grasp** how big he was. His clothing was so big that he had to use wagon wheels for buttons. Every time he took a step, he left a footprint so big it was the size of a lake! In fact,

you know those ten thousand lakes up in Minnesota? Well, Paul Bunyan was walking around up north, and his footprints filled up with water and made all those lakes. Yep, that's right. He was that big.

That Paul Bunyan was strong too. He had such a heavy ax that when he was walking through

Arizona, dragging his ax behind him, he dug out the Grand Canyon. Yep. The Grand Canyon didn't exist before that.

When he camped over in Oregon and needed to put out his campfire, he piled humongous rocks on it. That's how Paul made Mount Hood. You can even go see Mount Hood for yourself.

The other thing you need to know is that Paul Bunyan was fast. He was so fast that when he blew out his lantern at night, he'd hop into bed before the flame even went out. That's how fast he was.

When Paul Bunyan was born, it took five of the strongest storks to deliver him to his parents. He grew so fast that when he was a week old, he was big enough to wear his father's clothing. And every day he grew another foot taller! Paul was always hungry. It took ten cows to get enough milk for him. And even after eating forty bowls of oatmeal for breakfast, he was still hungry.

To rock him to sleep, his father had to use a lumber wagon and drive it to the top of a mountain and back. When he grew too big for

Lumber wagon

the wagon, his parents put him on a raft in the sea. But when the raft rocked back and forth, it made huge waves that sank ships for miles around.

Paul's folks didn't know what to do with the boy. Everything was too small for him. Everything but the great outdoors. So, he spent the rest of his life outdoors.

When Paul grew up, he became the greatest lumberjack around. He ran a logging camp with seven other lumberjacks almost as big as he was. All seven of them had the name Elmer. That way, whenever he needed anything, he just had to call "Elmer," and all of them came running.

## Tall Tales

The story of Paul Bunyan is a "tall tale," or a story about a person that is bigger than life. Everything about a tall tale is bigger or faster or more than real life. That is what makes the story funny.

The Paul Bunyan tale is a famous American tall tale. It began in the 1800s among lumberjacks in the forests of the northern United States.

Lumberjacks enjoyed spending hours telling about Paul Bunyan. Each man took turns making up things about Paul Bunyan. Each wanted his tale to be bigger and better than the last. It was like a game, and everybody pretended the tale was real.

But if a storyteller was skilled enough and the story was told well enough, the listeners just had to laugh.

Over time, lots of different tales about Paul Bunyan developed in different places. For the lumberjacks, who had tough, dangerous jobs, these tales helped make life more fun and more interesting.

To the lumberjacks, Paul Bunyan became a symbol of strength and greatness.

Those lumberjacks ate a lot too, but Paul ate the most. He kept the camp cook hopping; he ate 500 pancakes for breakfast each morning!

Well, years ago we had a winter that was so cold that when you milked your cow, the milk turned into ice cream before it hit the pail. The boiling coffee froze so fast it was still hot when it was frozen. And when folks talked, the sounds froze right in the air. After spring came and everything thawed, the chatter was heard for weeks!

That winter, it snowed so much that the snow covered most of the treetops. It was a lot of snow. When Paul Bunyan was out walking around in that deep snow, he spotted itty bitty ears sticking up out of the snow. He thought a poor animal had gotten stuck, so he pulled it out. It turned out to be a baby ox. Paul felt sorry for the poor thing, so he put it in his pocket and took it home. He fed the baby ox

Lumberjacks around 1900
Kerry & Co / Tyrrell Photographic Collection

warm milk, and then it curled up in front of the fire. Paul named the ox Babe and kept it for a pet.

Well, I never knew why, but Babe just started growing and growing. It was just like when Paul was a baby. If you looked at that ox for a few moments, you saw it growing right in front of you. Yep, Babe grew that fast.

When spring came, Paul put Babe in a

At least nine towns across the northern United States claim to be Paul Bunyan's birthplace! This monument of Paul Bunyan is in northern Minnesota.

barn for the night. But the next morning, Babe had vanished, and so had the barn! Paul looked and looked for his pet. After a while, he found Babe near a river, calmly eating grass. The funny thing was, that barn was still on top of him. It was stuck right on his back! Babe had outgrown the barn overnight.

Keeping Babe fed and watered wasn't easy. Babe ate a ton of grain for each meal. Then he went and pestered the cook for more. Paul had to dig great big watering holes for Babe. In fact, those watering

Babe the ox

holes turned into the Great Lakes. Yep, that's right. That's how the Great Lakes got made.

Babe was a great help for Paul. As fast as Paul chopped down logs, Babe hauled them over the logging roads and brought them to the mill. But the roads had way too many twists and turns. So Paul hooked Babe up to the far end of each road, and Babe pulled and pulled until the road was all smoothed out. When he was finished, he had twenty miles of extra road left over. So, Paul made a new logging road with the extra miles.

Babe liked pulling loads in winter best. In winter, snow and ice covered the roads and made them smooth. After the spring thaw, Paul had his men paint the roads white. That way, Babe thought it was still winter and kept on hauling through the summer.

Last I heard, Paul was off in California. Or maybe it was Alaska — you never can tell. Folks say he

Another Paul Bunyan monument in northern Minnesota

shows up in Minnesota every now and then, too. But don't count on it. He keeps to the forests, and it always seems that each time you hear about him, you just missed him. Too bad, you know... that Paul Bunyan, he is quite a sight.

| | |
|---|---|
| chocolate | c̲h̲oc ō lāt̲e̲ |
| average | av e̲r̲² ag̲e̲ |
| American | Ā mĕr i can |
| consumes | con sūm̲e̲s² |
| removes | rē möv̲e̲s² |
| factory | fac t̲or̲⁴ y |
| separates | sep ā rāt̲e̲s |
| cultivate | cul ti vāt̲e̲ |
| cinnamon | cin² nā mon |
| continued | con tin ūe̲d² |
| ingredients | in grē di³ ents |
| businesses | bus² i ness e̲s̲ |
| diseases | di² s̲ea̲s² e̲s̲² |
| motivated | mō ti vā t̲e̲d |

# The Story of Chocolate

The average American **consumes** twelve pounds of chocolate each year! But how much do you know about chocolate? What is in chocolate? How is it made? Who makes it? You might be surprised what you can learn about this popular treat!

## Cocoa or cacao?

**Cacao** (cä cä ō) was the original word and spelling. Like many words, it changed with time. The spelling **cocoa** (cō coa) probably began when early English traders misspelled the word *cacao*. Today, *cacao* mostly refers to the trees and the seeds. *Cocoa* mostly refers to the powder that is made from the seeds.

## From Cacao Trees to Chocolate Candy

Chocolate is made from the seeds of the cacao tree. Cacao trees grow in warm, humid rainforests. Although cacao trees first grew in South America, today western Africa has the most cacao tree farms.

The cacao tree produces a fruit called a

Cacao pods

cacao pod. A cacao pod is about the size of a coconut and has points on each end, like an American football. A farmer picks the pods off the tree and opens them up. Inside the pod, thick white

Cacao seeds surrounded by thick, white pulp

pulp surrounds 30-50 seeds, or cacao beans. This is enough to make about 7 bars of milk chocolate or 2 bars of dark chocolate. The farmer removes the cacao beans from the pod and lets them sit for a week to bring out the chocolate flavor. Then the farmer spreads them out in the sun to dry. Afterward, the dry beans get shipped to a chocolate factory.

The chocolate factory roasts, shells, and grinds up the cacao beans. Then the ground up cacao beans go through a process that separates the cocoa powder

Cacao pods with seeds

# The History of Chocolate

Chocolate was discovered around 1500 BCE in the Amazon rainforest of South America. The Mayans (600 BCE) and the Aztecs (400 CE) began to cultivate cacao trees. The cocoa was used to make a bitter, unsweetened drink.

In 1528, a Spanish explorer named Cortez brought cocoa back to Spain. The Spanish added sweetener, vanilla, and cinnamon. The king and his court enjoyed the drink so much, it became the secret drink of the Spanish Court.

In the 1600s and 1700s chocolate sales expanded. France, England, Italy, and the Netherlands began to open chocolate shops.

The process for making chocolate continued to change and develop. In the 1800s, chocolate makers discovered how to turn chocolate into a solid and make chocolate candy. Later, milk chocolate was created by adding powdered milk to it. By the early 1900s, lots of different businesses had started making chocolate. Chocolate became popular around the world.

(the part of the seed that has the chocolate flavor) from the cocoa butter (the part of the seed that is a fat). Finally, the cocoa powder is sweetened and mixed with other ingredients such as milk powder and turned into chocolate candy.

## The Chocolate Industry Today

Chocolate is popular all around the world. This means producing chocolate is a big **industry**. If a company can convince **consumers** to purchase its chocolate, that company can get very rich. Each company competes with many others to sell more chocolate and make more profit. In order to make the most profit, a company needs to sell a lot of chocolate. The company also needs to keep its own cost of making chocolate low.

Cacao beans drying in the sun

Sadly, many businesses that make chocolate keep costs low by mistreating the cacao bean farmers. Many farmers get paid such a small amount for the cacao beans that it is difficult for them to pay for enough food and decent housing.

In many places, school

is not free. When the farmers are not paid well enough for the cacao beans, the farmers cannot afford to send children to school. In fact, many children have no choice but to work on the family cacao farm all day, every day, just to help the family pay for food and housing.

At times, children even get taken from home to live and work as slaves on cacao farms. The children work long, hard hours every day, without being allowed to go home.

Cacao trees grow best and produce the most cacao beans when surrounded by a rainforest. The shade provided by other trees and the rainforest animals help the cacao trees grow well and protect them from diseases. Sadly, however, many farmers have destroyed parts of the rainforest in order to plant more cacao trees, not realizing the problems that result in the end.

Since the children do not get paid, businesses do not have to pay as much for the cacao beans. The businesses can then sell the chocolate more cheaply, so more consumers purchase it. But it is cheap at a great cost to the children.

However, other businesses work hard to treat workers fairly. The workers get paid fair wages. This allows them to have decent homes and good food. And the workers can afford to send children to school. On these farms, nobody is a slave. In order to do this, the company has to pay the farmers more for the cacao beans. This means it costs the company more to make the chocolate. And it costs the consumer more to purchase the chocolate.

Each time chocolate is purchased, the consumer makes a choice. The consumer chooses to purchase chocolate from a company that treats its workers fairly or to purchase chocolate from a company that pays poor wages. These choices have a huge impact on the businesses that make chocolate and on the lives of cacao farmers.

Cacao seeds, partly shelled

When a consumer purchases chocolate from a company that is not treating its workers fairly, the company is not motivated to change. When consumers stop purchasing chocolate from businesses that do not treat workers fairly, those businesses need to change or the company will not have customers. But many consumers do not know how chocolate is produced, or how the company treats its farmers. Many consumers  just purchase whichever chocolate is cheapest.

However, when consumers decide to purchase chocolate from a company that treats its farmers and workers fairly, consumers can make a difference in the lives of cacao farmers. Many of these products have a Fair Trade label. The Fair Trade label means each person working to grow the cacao beans and make the chocolate is treated and paid fairly. As consumers have purchased more fair trade chocolate, businesses have started to notice that consumers care about the treatment of workers. Many businesses have even started to make changes.

Businesses, consumers, and farmers all need to work together to address the problems in the chocolate industry. Hopefully, life for cacao bean farmers will soon be as good as chocolate!

# Unit 18

| | |
|---|---|
| perilous | per i l<u>ou</u>s [4] |
| civil | c[2]iv il |
| officer | of fi c[2]<u>er</u> |
| opportunity | op p<u>or</u> tū ni ty[4] |
| trustworthy | trust <u>wor</u>th[2] y[4] |
| Confederate | Con fed <u>er</u> āt<u>e</u> |
| Union | Ūn ion[4] |
| nervously | n<u>er</u> v<u>ou</u>s[4] ly[4] |
| assignment | as sī<u>gn</u> ment |
| alarm | ā l<u>ar</u>m |
| beautiful | b<u>ea</u> ū ti fül |
| concerned | con c[2]<u>er</u>n<u>e</u>d[2] |
| approach | ap pr<u>oa</u>ch |

# A Perilous Escape
Based on a true story

## The American Civil War

The American Civil War took place between Union and Confederate states from 1861-1865. Slavery, which was common in the Confederacy (South) and unpopular in the Union (North), was a major controversy in the war. The fighting began when the Confederate army attacked Fort Sumter and took it over. Fort Sumter was a large fort at the entrance to the important harbor of Charleston, South Carolina. The Union army responded by setting up a blockade of ships near Fort Sumter, preventing ships in Charleston from going out to sea.

Robert's hand shook as he buttoned up the officer's jacket. It fit him perfectly, but it felt formal and stiff compared to what he normally wore as a slave. He took a deep breath in an attempt to calm his nerves. The officers must be snoring loudly about now, he thought. Staying on shore was against the rules for the officers, but the rare opportunity to relax at home was too tempting for them. Besides, Robert had always shown himself to be entirely trustworthy, so it had seemed fine to leave him in charge. Indeed, Robert knew the *Planter* — the biggest ship in the Charleston harbor — as well as any of them.

Robert pulled on the officer's straw hat and nodded to his fellow slaves, who turned to

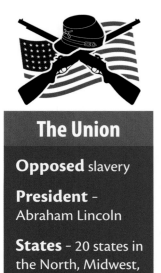

**The Union**

**Opposed** slavery

**President** -
Abraham Lincoln

**States** - 20 states in
the North, Midwest,
and West

start putting wood into the boiler. He opened the door of the pilothouse and stepped out onto the deck of the ship.

Robert had been waiting for this moment for so long, it was hard to think it was really happening. He had dreamed of the day of his escape to the **Union** North and of freedom from slavery. Robert and the others in the slave crew knew that in order to escape, several things needed to happen without a hitch.

First, the escape needed to take place on a night when the white officers decided to sleep on shore. The day before, as the crew had been loading

The *Planter* 1862

cannons to be brought to a new fort early the next morning, Robert had overheard the officers talking about staying on shore for the night. So this was it. Second, he and the other slaves on the *Planter* had family members that needed to be brought on board.

Between the harbor in Charleston and the Union blockade, five **Confederate** forts stood in the way, each equipped with cannons that might destroy the ship. Even if the *Planter* did manage to reach the Union blockade, the Union ships might think the *Planter* was an enemy ship, and shoot at it. It was an enormous risk, but he and the other slaves felt that freedom was worth it.

**The Confederacy**

**Supported** slavery

**President** - Jefferson Davis

**States** - 11 states in the South

"Seven miles," he thought, "just seven miles to the blockade, and then we will be free."

Robert heard the footsteps of the **sentry** on shore nearby. He hoped that with his officer's clothing and the darkness of the night, the sentry thought he was the white officer preparing his ship for an early-morning assignment. As the ship started leaving the harbor, he watched nervously to see if the sentry was at all alarmed. All was quiet. Robert took another deep breath.

Up the coast a short distance, he slowed down to a stop, and the crew waited for a little boat to pull up to the ship with the men's family members. As the women and children reached the deck, Robert

**Union Officer**

scooped up his beautiful little daughter, whispering to her that everything was going to be fine. He looked at his wife, Hannah, as she held his infant son, knowing that she was working hard to keep her own fears under control. Both of them knew that getting caught meant certain death.

When the *Planter* moved off again, Robert steered toward the first fort. As he got near, he was trembling with nervousness. But he calmly sounded the secret signal to announce his presence. After a pause, the sentry in the fort responded with another signal to say he was permitted to pass. He was careful not to travel too quickly, which might seem strange to the sentry. The *Planter* passed another fort, and another, and another, each time giving the secret signal and nervously waiting for the return signal from each fort.

**Confederate Officer**

As the ship approached the last fort, Fort Sumter, the sun was starting to rise.

Robert was concerned that the sentry at the fort might be able to see that he wasn't the white officer. He pulled the officer's hat down low on his head to shade his face and folded his arms across his chest as he had seen the officer do many times. The

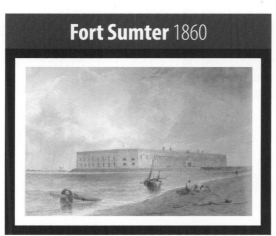

**Fort Sumter** 1860

*Planter* sounded the signal and waited, and waited. Finally the fort gave the signal saying the *Planter* was allowed to pass. Continuing slowly along the coast toward another fort, he carefully waited until the ship was out of range of Fort Sumter's cannons before turning and speeding toward the Union ships.

Getting ready for the final challenge of approaching the Union blockade, the crew members immediately replaced the Confederate flag

**Fort Sumter** 2014

**Ship similar to the *Onward***

with a white flag, which was a sign of surrender. As it reached the Union ships, however, the nearest ship, called the *Onward*, didn't see the white flag. Thinking it was an enemy ship coming to attack, the *Onward* sounded an alarm and got ready to shoot. But just before the command to fire, a sailor yelled out that he saw a white flag.

The *Onward* signaled to the *Planter* to move closer. As it approached, Robert leaned over the rail and yelled out to the captain, "Good morning, Sir! I have brought guns for the United States!" The *Onward's* captain stared open-mouthed in surprise as the crew of former slaves jumped up and down, cheering and yelling. When the ship's door burst open, several women and children ran out to the deck to join them and the captain of the *Onward* smiled.

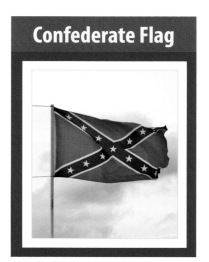

**Confederate Flag**

**Union Flag**

The former slaves begged him for a Union flag to put up on the *Planter*. As the flag was proudly hoisted up, Robert stepped over to embrace Hannah and the children. With tears running down her face, Hannah held up the baby boy, saying, "Look at that flag, Son. That flag means freedom. Your life will never be the same."

# Unit 19

| | |
|---|---|
| although | äl th͟ough |
| slavery | slā ver y |
| practice | prac tice |
| restaurant | rest au ränt |
| dependable | dē pend ā ble |
| increased | in creased |
| convinced | con vinced |
| money | mon ey |
| demonstrating | dem on strā ting |
| trustworthy | trust wor th͟y |
| confident | con fi dent |
| appeared | ap peared |
| attitudes | at ti tūdes |
| representative | rep rē sent ā tive |

# Robert Smalls

(1839-1915)

Robert Smalls was born as a slave in South Carolina in 1839. His mother was a house slave for the McKee family, and he too began working for them as a house slave when he was about six years old. He was a smart, cheerful boy. Although the McKee family treated him well compared to many other slaves, as he got older he began to understand how cruel slavery was, and he grew to hate it.

When Robert was twelve years old, Mr. McKee hired him out in the big harbor city of Charleston. This was a common practice with slaves at the time. Robert did work such as lighting the gas street lamps and waiting on tables in a restaurant. As his owner, Mr. McKee kept the money Robert earned.

Robert was smart and dependable, and he worked hard. As time went on, Mr. McKee gave Robert more choice in his jobs. Robert loved the waterfront, so he chose

Slaves working outside, about 1862

Charleston, 1865

to work at the docks, loading and unloading cargo from the ships that came and went. Later he made sails and got to test them on boats in the water. This is when he started to learn how to pilot a boat. As Robert's sailing skills increased, he was able to work as a sailor.

Meanwhile, in 1856 Robert fell in love with a woman named Hannah, who was also a slave. In order to marry, they had to work out an agreement with Hannah's owner as well as with Mr. McKee. In the agreement, Robert and Hannah had to pay their owners a set amount every month, and they could keep whatever extra money they earned.

Their first child, a daughter, was born in 1858. Since Hannah was still a slave, the daughter legally belonged to Hannah's owner. Robert had hated slavery and longed for freedom for a long time, but now he wanted it even more. Robert convinced Hannah's owner to agree to sell Hannah and their daughter to him for $800. It was a huge amount of money, but they worked hard to earn the money through taking on extra jobs. A couple of years later, they had a son as well.

In 1860, Robert joined the slave crew of the *Planter*, a 147-foot wood-burning steamer that hauled cotton. But when the Civil War started in 1861, the *Planter* and its crew were taken over by the Confederate navy. First Robert and the others on the ship worked to help improve defenses around Charleston and the surrounding area, such as laying mines and constructing forts. Then the *Planter* helped transport guns and troops to the new forts. After demonstrating that he was both skilled and trustworthy, Robert was promoted to wheelman, which meant he was in charge of steering the boat. Even though he had no choice but to help the Confederates, he really wanted the Union to win the war in the hope that slavery would end.

When the Union navy set up a blockade seven miles away from

The *Planter* hauling bales of cotton, about 1860

Charleston in 1862, Robert was able to see the Union ships from Charleston on clear days. Robert felt confident that reaching the blockade was his best hope of freedom for his family and himself.

Robert's escape took place in the early morning hours of May 13, 1862. When the *Planter* appeared in front of the Union ships, it was a big surprise. Not only was it incredible that the slaves had escaped, but Robert had also brought the Union four cannons, loads of explosives, a ship, and the valuable Confederate code book which contained secret signals and secret plans about the placement of mines in the area.

Robert Smalls,
between 1870 and 1880
Library of Congress: Brady-Handy Collection

In the North, Robert became famous for his daring escape. The *New York Times* said it was among "the most heroic acts of the war." His **exploits** certainly did not stop then. Robert served the Union as a pilot and captain and was involved in seventeen different battles.

Again he became known for being smart, brave, and skilled. Robert also had a significant influence in changing laws and attitudes that discriminated against African Americans, both during and after the war.

Robert Smalls grew up in this house as a slave. He later bought it and lived in it for the rest of his life.

Near the end of the war, Robert learned to read and write for the first time. After the war ended, he bought the same house he had lived in during his childhood as a slave, and he lived in it for the rest of his life. Robert became a political leader in South Carolina, serving in the South Carolina House of Representatives and State Senate and later the U.S. Congress. He fought long and hard for African American rights. Robert Smalls was the longest-serving African American congress member of his era.

# Unit 20

| | |
|---|---|
| familiar | fā mil i̲a̲r⁴ |
| delicate | del i cāt̲e̲ |
| beautiful | b̲e̲a̲ ū ti ful |
| practical | prac ti cal |
| surprised | s̲u̲r prī²s̲e̲²d̲ |
| sorrowfully | sor r̲o̲w² fül ly⁴ |
| chastised | c̲h̲as tī²s̲e̲²d̲ |
| argument | a̲r gū ment |
| aggravated | ag grav ā t̲e̲d̲ |
| terrible | ter ri bl̲e̲ |
| disgruntled | dis grunt l̲e̲²d̲ |
| defeated | dē f̲e̲a̲t̲ e̲d̲ |
| confidence | con fi denc̲e̲² |
| smirked | sm̲i̲r̲k̲e̲³d̲ |

# The Milkmaid, the Brothers, and the Lessons They Learned

## The Milkmaid and Her Pail

The pail was brimming with milk when Molly lifted it up carefully to balance it on top of her head. Then she waved at her mother and set off for the market.

As she walked along the familiar path, her mind started wandering. She thought about the dress she had seen at the dress shop in town. It was made

with shiny red satin and trimmed with delicate white lace. It had an enormous skirt that reached all the way down to the floor. It was the most beautiful dress that Molly had ever seen. She knew it was not very practical, but she wanted it more than anything in the world!

Then Molly started thinking about selling the milk. "Let's see. How much will I earn from selling this milk?" she thought. "With all that money, think of all the eggs I can get from Farmer Brown! When the eggs hatch, I will raise them until they are full-grown chickens. Then I can sell the chickens for even more money." Molly giggled with glee. "And with that money, I will get that beautiful dress!"

At this thought, Molly tossed her head back and laughed. But as she did, the pail fell off her head and the milk spilled out all over the ground.

"Oh, no!" she wailed. "Everything is ruined!" Molly wept as she looked at the wet ground. She thought about her plans for the chickens and the new dress, which were now destroyed. But weeping was not going to get the milk back, and she had no choice but to go home.

When she arrived, her mother was surprised to see her so early. Molly sorrowfully explained what had happened, and her mother shook her head in dismay. "Next time, Molly," her mother chastised her, *"don't count your chickens before they hatch!"*

## The Three Brothers and the Sticks

Jake's voice was getting louder, but so was Jack's. And when Jon started shouting his own ideas into the middle of the argument, Jake and Jack got louder still. In a matter of seconds, the air was clanging with so many bitter, angry words that their father felt his ears hurting. In a matter of minutes, the father knew, the three brothers were going to be **having it out** on the ground with their fists.

The fact was that these three boys were starting to fight a lot. They hadn't fought much when they were little, but now that they were big teenagers, they seemed to fight all the time. The father often urged them to stop, sometimes with angry words of his own, but it never seemed to help. The father didn't like having to listen to the bickering, of course, but it was more than that. The most frustrating thing for the father was that he knew that each boy had great talents that were wasted when they were fighting. He also knew that none of them was perfect, and they needed each other.

Jack was the oldest and he was faster than a housefly in the middle of summer. But Jack wasn't very smart or strong. Jon, the middle boy, was smarter than a wise old owl, but he wasn't very strong or fast. Jake, the youngest, was as big and strong as an ox, but he just wasn't very fast or smart.

When the boys fought, they each seemed to be able to target the others' weaknesses. Jake pounded his brothers with painful force. Jack darted in for punches and ran off by the time Jake and Jon were able to respond. Jon's remarks confounded and aggravated his brothers, and he found sneaky ways of **tripping both of them up** at the same time.

The boys always fought until all three felt terrible. What was the point of that? How was a father to help his sons truly understand what was at stake here?

This time, as he listened to their argument get more and more heated, the father sighed and looked around him. He spotted a bundle of sticks lying on the ground, and it gave him an idea.

"Jack!" he called. "Grab that bundle of sticks and bring it here!"

Jack ducked Jake's punch, snatched up the bundle, and dashed to his father. Jake and Jon stopped suddenly and looked at their father to see what he was doing.

"Jack, you're pretty fast. Can you quickly break this bundle of sticks in half for me?"

"Of course!" Jack answered. But when he grabbed the bundle at each end and **gave it his best shot**, it was too hard. He looked up at his father, disgruntled and surprised.

"Well, give them to Jon then. Jon, you're pretty smart; you can do it, can't you?" Jack passed the bundle of sticks to Jon, but Jon wasn't able to break them, either.

"Okay, then, Jake is strong enough. Give them to Jake." Jake smirked at his brothers as he took the bundle, ready to show them how much stronger he was. But as hard as he struggled, he also failed to break the bundle of sticks.

"What?" asked the father. "None of you can break these sticks? Are these sticks stronger than you are?" The boys looked down at their feet, embarrassed to be defeated by mere sticks.

Then the father took the bundle apart and handed each of his sons a single stick.

"Here," he said. "Now try."

The boys snapped each stick apart as easily as if they were twigs, and went on to snap the rest of the sticks in the same way. They laughed and looked at their father with confidence again. They were glad to know that they weren't defeated by sticks after all.

Then the father looked at each of his sons. "If you act as you did a few minutes ago, just **thinking of yourself** and **putting down** your brothers, you will be like a single stick, quickly and easily broken by anybody who comes along. But if you band together like the bundle of sticks, even your strongest enemy will not be able to break you. *Strength is found in unity.*"

| | |
|---|---|
| identity | ī den ti ty⁴ |
| rebel | rē bel |
| parasitic | par ā sit ic |
| unsuspecting | un sus pect ing |
| innocent | in nō² cent |
| deceptive | dē² cep tive |
| delicate | del i cāte |
| differently | dif fer ent ly⁴ |
| canopy | can ō py⁴ |
| unashamed | un ā shāmed² |
| consecrated | con sē crā ted |
| destiny | des ti ny⁴ |
| extremely | ex trēme ly⁴ |
| epiphyte | ep i phyte |

# An Open Letter to the Banyan Tree

Weren't you ever told that trees don't do that?

Roots are meant for underground,
    as everybody knows.
Yet you send yours spilling out the top,
    dangling in the air
  like a gathering of rope swings
    offering rides.
And when they finally reach the ground,
  they simply dig in
    and declare a new identity,
      as tree trunks.
Tree trunks!
  Whoever heard of such a thing?

Weren't you ever told that trees don't do that?
What was it that made you rebel?

Seeds are meant for dirt, of course,
  I know you know that too.
Yet you send out each seed like a **parasitic** spy,
  searching for an unsuspecting rooftop

or some other innocent tree.
The sweetness of those pale green **tendrils**
    embracing their host like delicate fingers
  cannot mask their **deceptive** plan
    to strangle and destroy.
You know and I know;
  we all know it's true.

Weren't you ever told that trees don't do that?
What was it that made you rebel?
What drove you to think so differently?

Forests are made up of *trees*, if you please;
  not *tree*, you know - see the difference?
Yet you insist on making a whole forest
    out of a single tree!
  How can you think that's alright?
You reach out as if you own the world,
  crawling along on roots and branches
    and trunks all entwined.
Stop trying so hard!
  Can't you please?

Weren't you ever told that trees don't do that?
What was it that made you rebel?
What drove you to think so differently?
What is it that gives you such **zeal**?

Life is meant to be hard;
  at least you never said otherwise.
Yet you stretch out your **canopy**
      in **unashamed** praise,
  displaying the triumph of growth and grace.
You offer a shady welcome to the weary or lonely -
      a life-giving refuge,
      a rambling playground,
      a stage for songs with wings,
      a **consecrated venue**
              for gathering, sharing, communing...
Because life has always been hard.

How did you know to do that?
What was it that made you choose this?
What drove you to think so differently?
What is it that gives you such zeal?
Have you always known your destiny?
Or did you just do your best to be yourself,
      and learn along the way?

# Banyan Trees

Banyan trees send roots right off their branches, hanging down and dangling in the air. After they grow long enough to reach the ground, they dig

The dangling roots of the banyan tree are great for playing and swinging.

into the soil and continue to grow. Then the original hanging root grows thicker and wider, just like a trunk. These roots that have turned into trunks are called **prop roots**. Prop roots provide more and more strength to the branches overhead. This allows the branches to spread out further. Sometimes the complex network of branches

Banyan tree with prop roots

and prop roots makes it confusing to tell which is the original trunk!

Some banyan trees grow to be extremely large and cover huge areas. The largest known banyan tree is in India. It is about 550 years old. It covers an area of 19,107 square meters and it has hundreds of prop roots. It is only a single tree, but it looks like a whole forest!

Vendors have set up a market under a banyan tree.

In rural areas in India and other places, many villages have a banyan tree in the center of town which serves as a gathering place for sitting, talking, relaxing, or setting up a market.

The banyan tree is an **epiphyte**, or a plant that grows on another plant. When an epiphyte seed lands in a crevice of another tree, it grows branches and roots that go up, down, and

Banyan growing on another tree

Banyan tree growing around an old temple in Cambodia

around, searching for the ground to dig its roots in. As it grows, a banyan can end up surrounding the entire original tree. When a banyan tree grows around another tree, the original tree slowly strangles and dies. It may then rot out until there is just a hollow column inside the banyan tree where

the first tree used to be. Animals love to find these holes and hide in them.

In Cambodia, banyan trees have covered an old temple complex which was abandoned about 400 years ago. During the hundreds of years of neglect since then, banyan trees and other epiphytes have grown over, in, and around the temple. Now the jungle seems to have reclaimed the area for itself!

Fresh figs

The banyan tree is a type of fig tree. The Common Fig is the type of fig we often eat. The banyan tree is sometimes called the Strangler Fig. Do you know why?

# Unit 22

| | |
|---|---|
| kneaded | <u>knea</u>d <u>ed</u> |
| savored | sā v<u>or</u><u>ed</u>[2] |
| possible | pos si bl<u>e</u> |
| imagined | i mag[2] in<u>ed</u>[2] |
| mesmerized | mes[2] m<u>er</u> īz<u>ed</u>[2] |
| unattainable | un at t<u>ai</u>n ā bl<u>e</u> |
| imaginary | im ag[2] i nā ry[4] |
| cinnamon | cin[2] nā mon |
| enthusiastically | en thū[2][3] si as tic al ly[4] |
| consoled | con sōl<u>ed</u>[2] |
| arguing | <u>ar</u> gū in<u>g</u> |
| profusely | prō fūs<u>e</u> ly[4] |
| announced | an n<u>ou</u>nc<u>ed</u>[2][3] |
| generosity | gen[2] <u>er</u> os i ty[4] |

# The Boy Who Wanted a Drum
Adapted from a Traditional Indian Folktale

In a small village in India lived a poor woman and her son. Every morning the boy walked to a forest to find firewood and brought it to his mother. Sometimes he had to walk a long way to find enough wood.

Every day his mother got up and made *parathas*. She ground up some grain and mixed the flour with water and salt. She kneaded the dough and formed it into small balls. Then she took each ball and flattened it into a circle, adding layers of oil and spices and folding it and flattening it over and over. Finally, she started a fire with the wood that the boy

had brought and cooked the *parathas* in a pan.

When she was done, she wrapped the *parathas* in clean cloth for the boy to take to the market to sell. She always made an extra little *paratha* for him to eat as he walked to the market. The boy loved its salty, spicy flavor. He always **savored** it slowly to make it last as long as possible.

The mother loved her son very much and she was proud of his kind, cheerful spirit. But she was too poor to buy nice clothes or toys for him, and she always wished that she had more to give him.

The boy knew his mother did her best for him, and he did not complain about being poor. For the most part, he didn't mind not having nice clothes or toys. But he did have a secret wish that he had never told his mother. He loved music and he loved dancing, but what he loved the most was to hear the beat of a drum. Sometimes when his mother was not around, he practiced drumming on whatever he found—a pot or his knee or even just the ground. He imagined that he was playing a big, booming drum, and he was **mesmerized** by the pulsing of the beats. More than anything in the world, he wished he had a drum.

He didn't tell his mother about his secret wish, because he knew she had no money to buy it for him, and he didn't want to make her sad with his **unattainable** dream. His mother had seen him practicing his imaginary drum, though, and had guessed his secret wish. But she, too, did not bring up the topic with him, knowing a drum was beyond her ability to provide for him. Wanting to give him something, though, the next day she made an extra large *paratha* for him, topping it with a sprinkle of cinnamon. When she gave it to him, his face lit up with delight. It was just a small gift, but he thanked her enthusiastically and her heart swelled with joy to see his humble, grateful attitude. The boy put the big *paratha* in his pocket, planning to savor it later on his walk.

As he walked along the path to the market, the boy came across a potter and his family. The potter's little girl was crying and refused to be consoled.

The boy imagined how hungry the girl might be, and he thought about the wonderful *paratha* in his pocket. As much as he was looking forward to eating it, he decided to offer it to the little girl. The girl looked up at him and smiled as she took it, and then hungrily started munching on it. Her parents were grateful for his kindness.

"We don't have money to give you," the father told the boy, "but please, take this pot that I made yesterday."

The boy didn't really want a pot, but he took it anyway and politely thanked the potter and his wife.

As he walked farther along the path to the market, the boy came across a washerman and his wife. The couple was arguing because their water pot had just broken.

"It's your fault," the husband was saying. "How are we supposed to boil water for washing clothes now?"

"It's not my fault; it's your fault!" replied the wife. "You left it balancing on that rock!"

The boy imagined how tired and frustrated the couple must be, and he wanted to help them.

ARTEKI / Shutterstock.com

"Here, take this pot instead," he said as he held it out to them.

The husband and wife suddenly stopped their argument and turned to him in surprise. They took the pot gratefully, even though they had no money to pay for it. The wife was so happy, though, that she took off her own scarf and insisted that he take it in return. The boy didn't really want a scarf, but he took it anyway and politely thanked the woman.

As he continued on the path to the market, the boy came across a horse-trader. The horse-trader spotted the colorful hand-woven scarf that the boy was carrying and exclaimed, "What a beautiful scarf! That is just what I've been looking for to give to my wife!"

The boy imagined the wife's happiness at receiving such a gift from her husband, and so he told the man to take it.

"Thank you! You are so kind! This will mean so much to her!" Then the man gave him a horse in return! The boy didn't really want a horse, but he took it anyway and politely thanked the man.

As he walked on and approached the market, the boy saw a large wedding party sitting in the shade of a banyan tree. He saw that they were dressed up in fine clothes, and many of them had instruments like flutes and drums. But instead of being noisy and happy, they looked sad. The boy asked them what was wrong.

"We are all ready to begin our wedding parade," said the bridegroom, "but the man who was to

bring my horse never came. Without a horse for me to ride, we cannot begin the parade, and the whole wedding will be ruined!"

The boy knew how important it was for the bridegroom to ride a horse in the wedding parade to the bride's house. He imagined how sad the bridegroom must be to be unable to begin his wedding, and how concerned the bride must be as she waited and waited for him to come.

"Here," he told the bridegroom. "Take this horse for your parade."

The man hardly dared to trust his ears, but he thanked the boy **profusely** and joyfully announced the great news to the rest of the wedding party.

"Please," said the man, "what can I give you in return for your generosity?"

"Well," said the boy, "what I really want, more than anything in the world, is a drum."

The man instantly called the drummers over to him and said, "Here! Pick whichever drum you want and I will buy it for you!"

The boy nearly burst with delight as he picked out a small hand drum that was easy to carry.

When he got to the market, the boy started calling out, just as he did each day, "*Parathas! Parathas! Parathas* for sale!" With all the noise and bustle of the market, though, nobody seemed to notice him.

The boy imagined what might make everybody want to listen, and he got an idea. He took his drum and started beating out a pattern. The deep, booming sound got faster and faster as he beat his drum, until his hands seemed to be flying. The shoppers started drifting over to him, nodding their heads in time to the beat, infected by the happy mood of the drum. In a short time, all the *parathas* were sold. The boy rushed home to tell his mother all about his drum and how he got it. When she heard his story, she threw back her head and laughed with joy. Then he played his drum for her, and as the other villagers heard it, they joined in as well, singing and dancing and twirling until late into the night.

| | |
|---|---|
| terrain | t<u>er</u> r<u>ai</u>n |
| encountered | en c<u>ou</u>nt <u>er</u>ed² |
| electricity | ē lec tri ci² ty⁴ |
| telephones | tel ē <u>ph</u>ōn<u>e</u>s² |
| ingenious | in² gē⁴ ni<u>ou</u>s⁴ |
| universal | ū ni v<u>er</u> sal |
| entertainment | en t<u>er</u> t<u>ai</u>n ment |
| membrane | mem brān<u>e</u> |
| urgent | <u>ur</u>² gent |
| clarify | clā ri fȳ |
| communicate | com mū ni cāt<u>e</u> |
| language | lan <u>g</u>ua²g<u>e</u>² |
| significant | sig ni fi cant |
| instrument | in strū ment |

# The Message of the Drum

*When a British man named John Carrington stepped out of a jungle in western Africa after hours of traveling over difficult terrain, he encountered the biggest surprise of his life: the people in the village already knew he was coming! How did they know? He hadn't arranged the trip ahead of time. They had no electricity, let alone telephones. (And this was long, long before cell phones existed!) Did somebody tell them he was coming? How was that even possible?*

It was just a short time ago, considering the whole history of the world, that people started using electricity. Imagine what life was like before that – before light bulbs or phones or computers or anything else that used electricity. What if you lived a few hundred years ago, and you really needed to talk to somebody who was far away? You might be able to send a letter with somebody who was traveling that way. Or, if you were very wealthy and important, like a king, you might even hire a messenger to carry the letter as fast as possible. Still, though, the message only traveled as fast as a person or maybe a horse was able to walk or run.

But what if the message was really urgent? Maybe you needed help, or you needed to send a warning that the river was flooding, or announce the arrival of an important person (or John Carrington!)... what then? In most places, it simply wasn't possible to send a fast message.

In some places, however, people figured out ingenious ways to communicate over a long distance. How? They used drums!

Drums are undoubtedly the oldest instrument in the world (besides the human voice, of course). Drums are also nearly universal – that is, they exist all over the world. They serve many different purposes. Some drums are just

A woman playing a drum for a dance
photo courtesy of Samaan Frajallah

In many countries in western Africa, people use a drum that is known in English as a **talking drum**. The body of a talking drum is made out of wood. The drum is carved into a shape that is wide at each end and narrow in the middle. A **membrane**, such as an animal hide, is stretched

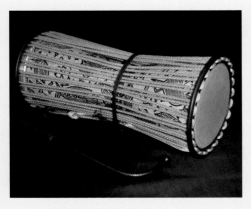

over each end of the drum. A long string or leather cord is strung around the outside of each membrane to connect them and hold them in place. When the membranes of the drums are stretched tightly over the end, the tone sounds higher. When they are looser, the tone sounds lower. With the cords, the drummer can control the tightness of the membranes and change the tone.

for musical entertainment. Some drums are used to keep everybody moving together at the same time, such as in a dance or a march. Sometimes a drum even performs an important role in a ceremony. But using a drum to talk? Carrington had never guessed that the villagers might use drums to communicate, but that's how they knew he was coming.

How did the drums "talk?" Have you ever said something like "I don't know" without opening your mouth? Try to hum "I don't know." Do you think someone could understand you? What about "I'm brushing my teeth?" (It probably helps if you have a toothbrush in your mouth!) In each phrase or sentence, certain words or syllables get more stress

– that is, they sound a little louder and longer than other words or syllables. The beats of a drum can imitate these different sounds. The sentence "I'm brushing my teeth" sounds like "Da-DUM-da-da-DUM."

In western Africa, however, there was something else significant about their languages that made drum messages possible. In those languages, different words have different **tones**. Different words can sound exactly the same in every way except that one is spoken up high, with a high tone, and the other is spoken down low, with a low tone. Likewise, drums can be made to have different tones. Drummers can then use the different tones of the drum to imitate the tones in words.

Of course, there are still bound to be certain words or phrases that have the same exact pattern.

In other places, people use a drum called a **slit gong**. A slit gong is made from a log – the bigger the log, the lower and louder the sound, and the farther the sound can travel. The middle of the log is hollowed out and a slit is carved along the side. To imitate the low and high tones of the language, they make a thin side and a thick side in the log. The thin side makes a low sound and the thick side makes a high sound.

So, drummers get around this problem by using longer phrases or sentences, rather than just single words. For example, instead of saying "water," which might sound just like "mother" on the drum, they might say, "water that flows in the river." They also clarify meaning by repeating themselves in slightly different ways. This often happens in spoken language, too – particularly

Talking drums
Paula Davis / Wikipedia.com

when understanding might be difficult. For example, when a mother is talking to her toddler, she might say something like, "Are you hungry? Do you want to eat some food? How about a snack?"

Drums communicate well partly because they can be loud – louder than the human voice, and louder than any other instrument. The sound they make can also carry over long distances. Some drums can be heard as far away as seven miles in a forested area or up to twenty miles on a flat plain! When an important message is "spoken," the village that hears it repeats it on their drums, telling it to the next village. The next village then repeats it on their drums, and it keeps getting passed on from village to village. In fact, drum messages have been known to travel over a hundred miles an hour in this way!

*John Carrington and his wife lived in western Africa for many years and learned all sorts of things from their African hosts. They loved the "talking" drums so much that they both learned to play them. In fact, even years later, when Mrs. Carrington wanted to call her husband home for dinner, she used the drum to deliver her message!*

# Unit 24

| | |
|---|---|
| Murray | M<u>ur</u> <u>ray</u> |
| New Hampshire | N<u>ew</u>    Hamp <u>shīre</u> |
| tremendously | trē men d<u>ou</u>s ly |
| curious | cū ri <u>ou</u>s |
| gadgets | gad gets |
| assembled | as sem bl<u>ed</u> |
| encouraged | en c<u>our</u> ag<u>ed</u> |
| advantage | ad van ta<u>ge</u> |
| opportunities | op p<u>or</u> tū ni ti<u>es</u> |
| urged | <u>urged</u> |
| determined | dē t<u>er</u> min<u>ed</u> |
| admirals | ad m<u>ir</u> als |
| continuous | con tin ū <u>ou</u>s |

# Grace Murray Hopper:
## Computer Pioneer

Grace Murray was born in 1906 in New York City. She was an active child. She loved the summers that her family spent on a lake in New Hampshire where she played games with her younger brother and sister, swam, and climbed trees.

As a child, Grace was tremendously curious and **relished** taking apart gadgets to see how they worked. When she was seven years old, she took apart a clock to figure out how it worked. When she was unable to put it back together, she found another clock to see how it was assembled. When she was unable to put that one back together, she found yet another clock to take apart. By the time she was finished, she had taken apart seven clocks! At that point her mother discovered what she was doing, and limited her to only one clock.

Although she was taught to sew and play the piano, which was common for many girls, her parents encouraged her to take advantage of all sorts of learning opportunities. Her father urged her not to be limited by only doing what was considered normal for girls. He taught her to believe in herself, to be determined, and to go after what she wanted.

Grace's mother was fond of math and shared that joy with her. In fact, Grace loved math so much that she went on to earn a Ph.D. in math. This was a rare accomplishment for anyone at that time, let alone a woman. She taught math in a university, which was also rare for women in those days.

In 1930 she married Vincent Hopper, and she became Grace Murray Hopper.

When the U.S. entered World War II, Grace Murray Hopper joined the Navy. The Navy was working on a project at Harvard University to create a new kind of machine to help them make accurate calculations during battles. Hopper worked with a man named Howard Aiken, who developed a computer called Mark I. The Mark I, one of the first computers ever built, was eight feet high, two feet deep, and fifty-one feet long. It weighed 10,000 pounds, and contained 765,000 parts, including 500 miles of wire. It was controlled by rolls of paper tape with holes punched in it, and it had the ability to add, subtract, multiply, and divide. As one of its first programmers, Hopper had the joy of "playing" with the biggest gadget she had ever seen!

One day the Mark I computer was having a problem - it kept shutting down every few seconds. Suddenly, some **admirals** showed up who wanted to watch the computer work. Not wanting the admirals to know there was a problem, Hopper

Mark I

leaned against the computer and kept her finger on the start button to keep the computer running. The admirals never noticed the computer's continuous mistakes, and left thinking it was working perfectly!

After World War II, Hopper continued working with the team at Harvard University as part of the Navy Reserve, which was then working on making the Mark II. One day the Mark II computer was not working, and Hopper and her staff were struggling to figure out what was wrong. Finally she located the problem. A moth was stuck in the computer. She used tweezers to pull it out, then taped the bug

Moth taped to the log book
U.S. Naval Historical Center

to the log book. From that incident, Hopper coined the term "bug" to describe a computer problem, and the corresponding term "debug" to describe fixing a computer problem.

At that time, computers were only used by technical experts, but Hopper wanted other people to be able to use computers as well. In 1949, Hopper designed the first electronic computer that was intended for business use. It was called the UNIVAC I. It operated a thousand times faster than the Mark I. Businesses used it to calculate things like billing and salaries.

Grace Murray Hopper and UNIVAC

One of the reasons computers were so difficult to use is that people needed to use a complicated code to "talk" to the computer. So, Hopper developed a program that "translated" words into a machine code that the UNIVAC understood. It was very limited and was only able to handle twenty words, but Hopper felt certain that it was a great start. She wanted to expand it into an entire programming "language." She was told, however, that this was not possible.

It took three years before her idea was finally

accepted. She then led a team to develop the world's first computer language, COBOL. Her work on COBOL was ground-breaking and drastically changed the computer industry. Suddenly all sorts of people wanted to use computers for things like salaries, billing, and record-keeping. Hopper's

Grace Murray Hopper
U.S. Navy

work also allowed for many other developments in computing, including many systems and programs that are still used today.

Hopper reluctantly retired in the late 1960s. Six months after her retirement, however, the Navy asked her to return on a temporary assignment. That assignment lasted another twenty years! She also became a speaker, writer, and consultant. She told people not to fear change and to be open-minded. She encouraged people to work together, share ideas, try new things, and take chances.

Hopper received many awards and honors during her lifetime. Her first was in 1969, when she was the

USS Hopper
U.S. Navy

very first person to be voted as "Man of the Year" in computing. In 1983, she was given the rank of admiral in the U.S. Navy. Four years after her death in 1992, the USS Hopper, a military ship named in her honor, was launched. It was nicknamed "Amazing Grace."

| | |
|---|---|
| Iditarod | Ī dit ā rod |
| regularly | reg ū l<u>ar</u> ly⁴ |
| plunges | plun² ges² |
| mushers | mü<u>sh</u> <u>er</u>s² |
| deprive | dē prīv<u>e</u> |
| contestants | con tes tants |
| enthusiastically | en <u>th</u>ū²³ si as tic al ly⁴ |
| appropriate | ap prō pri āt³<u>e</u> |
| terrain | t<u>er</u> r<u>ai</u>n |
| Anchorage | An <u>ch</u>or² ag<u>e</u>² |
| treacherous | tr<u>each</u>² <u>er</u> <u>ou</u>s⁴ |
| commemorates | com mem ō rāt<u>e</u>s |
| diphtheria | dip<u>h</u> <u>th</u>ē ri³ ä |
| antitoxin serum | an ti³ tox in sē rum |

# Iditarod:
## The Toughest Race on Earth

A musher racing with a dog sled team in Alaska

It is a dog sled race that covers hundreds of miles of ice and snow, crossing mountains, valleys, and frozen rivers. The thermometer regularly plunges far below zero, and the wind sometimes blows the snow so hard that mushers cannot see their hands in front of their faces, let alone the trail they're trying to follow. Day after day, these men and women deprive themselves of sleep and risk frostbite, moose attacks, and countless other dangers. They place their lives in the hands of dogs. And yet, each year seventy or more contestants and their dog teams enthusiastically brace themselves for one of the world's longest, hardest races: the Iditarod!

The word *Iditarod* is a Native Alaskan word meaning "great distance," which seems appropriate for a sled dog race that covers more than 1,100 miles. Since it first began in 1973,

Musher leaving Anchorage at the start of the 2007 Iditarod
Matt Cooper / Shutterstock.com

the Iditarod has taken place each year in March. It covers all sorts of terrain, following historic mail trails from the city of Anchorage in southern Alaska to the town of Nome in Alaska's far northwestern corner. Both men and women compete with their dogs, typically taking ten to twenty days to complete the race.

Mushers, or sled dog drivers, spend years

Sled dog puppy

preparing to compete in the Iditarod. Many raise their own dogs, training them to be sled dogs from the time they are puppies. The puppies must learn

Sled dogs are high energy dogs with a strong drive to run and pull.

to obey commands and work together on a team. They also practice running more and more miles each day. During the Iditarod, the dogs must be able to run 100 miles a day.

As the big race draws near, mushers pack their sleds carefully. They try to keep the sled as light as possible to make it easier for the dogs to pull it. They need a lot of things to survive the race, though: a sleeping bag, snowshoes, an ax, a small burner and fuel, a headlamp, and food. Most of the food can be sent ahead of time to checkpoints along the way, so they only need to carry a small amount with them on their sled. In the Iditarod, mushers must also bring a package of mail to deliver to Nome, symbolizing the historic role of mail carriers in Alaska.

# Mushing

Mushing, or driving a sled dog team, has existed for hundreds of years. The original purpose of mushing was not for fun or sport, but for work. Native Alaskans used sled dogs for traveling and hauling heavy loads.

During the late 1800s and early 1900s as Alaska was being settled by newcomers, in many areas sled dogs were the only reliable way to get around in the winter. A network of trails, called the Iditarod Trail, was established along some trails that had been made long ago by native Alaskans.

One of the most important uses of these trails was for mail. A large relay of mail carriers used their sled dogs to transport mail. Each musher would carry the mail for thirty miles or more from one town or roadhouse to the next, and then pass it off to the next musher. For many Alaskans, this mail was their one and only link to the outside world during the winter, and these mail carriers were greatly respected.

After airplanes could be used in Alaskan winters, they

Mushers must prepare for all sorts of weather. On the trail, it can be as cold as 50 degrees below zero! If it is also windy, the wind chill can be perhaps 100 degrees below zero! The dogs have thick fur coats to protect them from the cold. The dogs wear boots to protect their feet from the sharp ice.

If blowing snow makes it hard to see, a musher must rely on the lead dog, or the first dog on the team, to find the trail with its nose.

Surprisingly, one of the biggest problems during the Iditarod is when the weather is too warm. When the temperatures rise above freezing, the dogs overheat in their

started replacing the sled dog mail carriers. Later, snowmobiles replaced more sled dogs. By the 1960s, mushing had nearly died out.

The first Iditarod race was held in 1973 and marked a renewed interest in mushing – now not simply as a means of transport, but as a sport. In recent years, mushing has become increasingly popular, and the Iditarod, the world's longest sled dog race, is now famous world-wide.

thick fur coats, and they cannot run as fast! Also, the warm sun turns the trail into slush. That makes it hard to pull the sled, and the dogs get all wet and muddy.

Besides the weather, Iditarod contestants face other challenges on the trail as well. The surface of the trail can have slippery ice, deep snow drifts, or rocks and sticks that can poke up and injure the dogs' paws. In some places, the trail twists and bends through thick forests and treacherous mountainsides, so mushers must be careful to avoid crashing into trees or flying off of cliffs. In other places, the trail crosses creeks that may or may not be frozen. They can also encounter dangerous wildlife like wolves, bears, and moose.

Although the dogs have the main work of pulling the sled, the musher has a big job, too. The musher calls out commands to the dogs to go faster or slower or turn, and makes choices about when to go and when to stop and rest. Sometimes they help out their dogs by running behind the sled and pushing it from behind, like when they are going uphill. The sled can also flip over around turns or on slanted trails, so the musher helps keep the sled upright and balanced by leaning to the side or even sticking a foot out to help. Throughout the race, though, mushers put their dogs first, caring

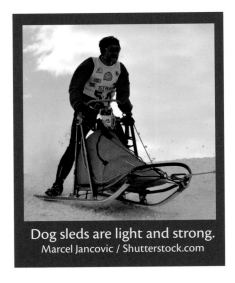

Dog sleds are light and strong.
Marcel Jancovic / Shutterstock.com

for them and giving them whatever they need.

Dotted along the trail are about twenty-six checkpoints where mushers must stop. At the checkpoints, mushers feed and rest their dogs. To give their dogs water, they might need to draw water from a hole in the ice or melt snow over a fire. They also check each dog for any problems, like hurt paws. Then they lay out hay for the dogs

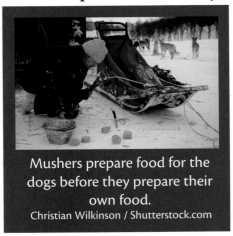

Mushers prepare food for the dogs before they prepare their own food.
Christian Wilkinson / Shutterstock.com

to sleep on. After all the dogs' needs have been met, the mushers can take a short rest themselves.

Between being on the trail and the time they spend caring for the dogs, Iditarod mushers themselves get very little sleep during the race. They take naps at some of the checkpoints or along the trail, or sometimes even while riding on the sled! They need to be

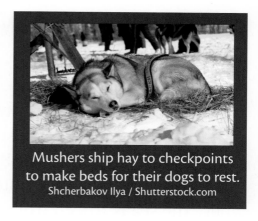

Mushers ship hay to checkpoints to make beds for their dogs to rest.
Shcherbakov Ilya / Shutterstock.com

careful not to fall off, though; if they do fall off the sled, the dogs will probably keep running, and then the only thing the musher can do is walk toward the next checkpoint, hoping to meet the dogs along the way!

Even though each musher is competing against all the other mushers, in another sense they are really competing together against the many challenges of the race. For many contestants, their goal is simply to finish the race, which is an enormous accomplishment itself. According to racers, the Iditarod is one of the most exhausting yet amazing experiences of their lives. They love being out on the beautiful trail, they love being with their dogs, and they love the challenge. As one musher put it, "It's funny, but most of the people who run the Iditarod, no matter how rough they've had it, want to go back and do it again."

# Saving Nome

The Iditarod **commemorates** one of the most significant and memorable stories about mushing in Alaska: the Great Serum Run to Nome in 1925. Nome is in the far northwestern part of Alaska, where the sea is frozen from November to June, preventing ships from being able to go in and out during those months. Although the town was mostly isolated from the outside world in the early 1900s, they did receive mail, delivered by dog sleds. The mail would be sent part of the way by train, and where the track ended in Nenana, mushers would take turns relaying the mail 674 more miles to Nome. The whole trip normally took about twenty-five days.

In January of 1925, there was an outbreak of

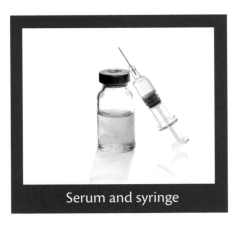

Serum and syringe

**diphtheria** in Nome. Diphtheria was extremely contagious and killed nearly everyone who got it. Children were particularly vulnerable, and often died within a day or two of getting

Map of the Iditarod Trail and the 1925 serum run
U.S. Bureau of Land Management

the disease. As soon as the people realized what was happening, they were terror-stricken. They had fresh memories of another outbreak of a disease that had occurred only seven years earlier. Over 1,000 people in the town and surrounding areas had died, including half of the native Alaskan population. They knew that in a matter of two weeks, this new disease could **devastate** the entire town. Besides the 1,400 people living in Nome in 1925, another 10,000 people living in the surrounding areas were threatened as well. Everyone was terrified.

The only chance for survival was to get the

**antitoxin serum** that could stop the progress of the disease. The doctor in Nome sent out a panicked telegraph to request the serum, which was available in Anchorage. But getting it to Nome in winter was a problem. In the time it would normally take for the train and sled dogs to bring it, the town could already be wiped out.

With no other choice, the town leaders made a plan to use a relay of the fastest mushers they could find. In the end, twenty different mushers participated in the relay to get the serum to Nome. The sled dog teams included over 160 dogs.

Knowing that every minute that passed before

the serum arrived could mean another life was lost, the mushers in the relay raced as fast as they possibly could, many of them pressing on in conditions that were far worse than what they would normally travel through. At the time of the serum run, Alaska was experiencing a winter that was colder than it had been in twenty years. On some parts of the trail it was 63 degrees below zero, far colder than the -40 degrees that they normally considered acceptable for sled dogs.

Many of the mushers experienced life-threatening conditions. One musher's face was partly black from frostbite when he arrived at his stopping point. Another musher's hands froze onto the handle of his sled, and someone had to pour water over them to get them loose. In some places the snow was blowing so hard that they could not see a short distance in front of them. The mushers depended entirely on their lead dogs to find the trail.

In the end, the whole trip took only five and a half days, which was considered miraculous, and the town of Nome was saved.

# Unit 26

| Leonhard | L<u>eo</u>n <u>h</u>ard |
|---|---|
| Seppala | Sep pä lä |
| pouncing | p<u>ou</u>n c<sup>2</sup>ing |
| enthusiasm | en <u>th</u>ū<sup>2 3</sup> si<sup>2</sup> asm |
| marveling | m<u>ar</u> vel i<u>ng</u> |
| persistence | p<u>er</u> sist enc<u>e</u><sup>2</sup> |
| obviously | ob vi<sup>3</sup> <u>ou</u><sup>4</sup>s ly<sup>4</sup> |
| agitating | ag i<sup>2</sup> tā ti<u>ng</u> |
| immediately | im mē di<sup>3</sup> āt<u>e</u> ly<sup>4</sup> |
| audacity | <u>au</u> dac<sup>2</sup> i ty<sup>4</sup> |
| tenacity | ten ac<sup>2</sup> i ty<sup>4</sup> |
| island | ī<u>s</u> land |
| diphtheria | di<u>ph</u> <u>th</u>ē ri<sup>3</sup> ä |
| undoubtedly | un d<u>oub</u>t <u>ed</u> ly<sup>4</sup> |

# Togo

"**W**hat's going on?" Leonhard Seppala exclaimed. As a musher with a kennel full of dogs, Sepp, as his friends called him, was used to hearing a lot of barking. But this racket was different. He stepped outside to investigate, and there was Togo, jumping around, barking and wagging his tail, obviously thrilled to be back home.

"How did you get here?" Sepp often talked to his dogs as if they could understand him perfectly. "I sold you to someone miles away. How did you escape?" Togo responded by joyfully pouncing on Sepp, nearly knocking him to the ground in his enthusiasm.

It turns out that Togo had escaped by jumping through his new owner's big front window before

finding his way back to his birthplace at Sepp's. Sepp shook his head, marveling at the dog's persistence. "Well, if you want to be here that bad, I guess you can stay."

Sepp decided he wouldn't try to sell Togo

again, but he didn't know what to do with him, either. Togo had been a problem since the day he was born. The only pup in his litter, he had been small and sickly. Sepp's wife Constance had taken over the job of nursing him back to health. Togo got through it, but he always remained smaller than the other dogs—too small to be a good sled dog.

Besides, Togo was a trouble-maker. He was constantly escaping and getting in the way. Whenever Sepp tried to harness a dog team, Togo would run around and nip at the other dogs' ears. At other times, Togo would try to chase down other animals or charge after other dog teams.

Togo just wasn't cut out for real work. And Sepp had plenty of work to do with his sled dogs. He traveled as many as 7,000 miles a year, checking on his boss's gold mines. Sepp was a tough driver, too. While other mushers considered thirty miles to be a full day's run, Sepp often traveled fifty to a hundred miles in one day with his dogs. He needed dogs that took their job seriously and worked hard. Obviously, that wasn't Togo.

So, when a woman had come by to buy a dog for a pet, Sepp hadn't thought twice about offering Togo. Now that Togo was back, though, Sepp decided he might as well let him stay, figuring he might be useful for something someday. He just hoped the dog wouldn't cause too much trouble in the meantime.

Togo didn't quit. He kept getting loose, agitating the other dogs, and charging after reindeer. One day, though, Togo convinced Sepp that he too was ready to work. When Sepp hitched up a dog team and took off on a ten-day mail run, Togo  barked wildly from where he was tied up behind the seven foot wire fence. Later that night, as a blizzard was beginning to bear down, Togo decided to make another escape. He wrestled loose from his ropes, backed up, and took a running leap over the fence – and almost made it. One of his back legs got caught on the top of the fence, and when the caretaker came out to see what the howling was about, he saw Togo hanging upside-down. The caretaker helped loosen Togo's leg, and Togo immediately dashed away, bleeding leg and all. Several hours and thirty-three miles later, Togo managed to track down Sepp and the rest of the team.

Once again, Sepp shook his head and marveled at Togo's audacity. He bandaged the dog's foot, wondering if he would be able to keep up on the long distance he still needed to go. Sepp let Togo run beside the sled. But just as he always had, Togo ran around and distracted the other dogs. So Sepp hitched up Togo right in front of his sled where he could keep him in his sight. To his surprise, Togo suddenly stopped being wild and crazy and focused on his job of pulling. Togo was even better than his teammates! Sepp decided to move Togo further up in the line. Again, Togo surprised Sepp with his strength and tenacity. Sepp kept moving Togo up the line further and further until by the end, he was sharing the lead. On Togo's very first sled dog trip, he went seventy-five miles, pulling harder than any of the other dogs the whole way.

As Togo was given the opportunity to show what he could do, it turned out that he made an excellent lead dog. Being a lead dog was the hardest, most important job on the team. The lead dog had to respond to the musher's commands, keep the team on the right trail, and set the pace. The lead dog had to be determined enough to push ahead in the midst of bitterly cold, fierce winds when most dogs would stop, and smart enough to see and hear dangers that the musher might not be able to notice from his place in back. As long as there was a good lead dog, the other dogs would follow. But it all depended on the lead dog.

Before long, Togo became Sepp's favorite lead dog. Togo even helped Sepp win several consecutive sled dog races. Soon Sepp and Togo became known as the fastest sled dog team in Alaska.

Togo was not just fast, though; he was also smart and brave. One of the most dangerous parts of mushing was crossing frozen rivers, lakes, or even sea inlets. Sometimes there were cracks that threatened to open up and swallow the team, or deceptively slippery spots that could throw a team out of control. The musher had to concentrate very hard on listening for cracking sounds or watching for changes in the ice to avoid. But the musher also had to rely on his lead dog, who was in many ways the true guide, leading the team forward or turning to avoid a soft spot. Togo saved the team from disaster time and time again.

The most dangerous part of the trail was the part that crossed over the Norton Sound. The Norton Sound was an inlet in the sea that was so far north that the water completely froze during the winter. Crossing the forty-two miles over the frozen sound saved a whole day of travel time, but it was also risky. Apart from the other dangers of traveling over frozen water, it was always possible for a large chunk of ice to break away from the shore and drift into the sea.

According to Sepp, one day when he and his

dog team had nearly finished crossing the Norton Sound, the worst possible thing happened. The large chunk of ice that Sepp and his team were traveling on suddenly broke away from the shore, leaving Sepp and the dogs stranded on an island of ice. The wind was blowing away from the shore, pushing the floating island farther and farther away. There was nothing Sepp could do but sit and watch, knowing there was little chance that he would survive. Hours later, though, hope returned when the wind changed and started blowing his floating island closer to the shore again. When it got to be about five feet away, perhaps as close as it was going to get, Sepp had an idea. He hooked up Togo to a long rope, picked him up, and threw him across the gap. Togo, who seemed to understand perfectly well why he'd just been thrown through the air, landed and started pulling on the rope, slowly bringing the island closer to shore. But then the rope suddenly broke, leaving the end dangling in the water! Sepp looked at Togo in shock, realizing his last hope had just disappeared. But what happened next turned out to be the biggest shock of all: Togo jumped into the freezing water, grabbed the broken rope, and scrambled back up on shore. Again, he pulled and pulled on the rope. Inch by inch, the gap started closing, until Sepp and the rest of the team were able to leap to the other side as well.

Of all of Togo's brave acts, though, the one he will always be remembered the most for was his last, which was during the 1925 Serum Run to Nome. When the diphtheria outbreak occurred and antitoxin serum was located in Anchorage, Sepp was instructed to immediately leave Nome with his sled dog team and meet another musher at a half-way point between Nome and the train stop where the serum would be picked up. After Sepp left, though, more arrangements were made so that other mushers could join them in a relay and make it go even faster.

Sepp didn't know that other dog teams were helping out, however. Undoubtedly thinking of his eight-year-old daughter and all the others that were threatened by diphtheria back home, he pressed on as hard as he could. When he had to make a choice about whether to cross the Norton Sound or go around it, he took the risk and crossed it. Not long after he made it to the other side, he was surprised to encounter another musher, whose dogs were tangled up in their ropes. Feeling the need to go as fast as possible, he told Togo to lead them around the other team, so they too wouldn't get tangled up. But then he heard shouting. "Serum!" yelled the other musher. "I have the serum!" Sepp screeched his team to a halt and ran to meet the other musher. Then he tied the bundle to his sled, swung his team around, and raced back in the other direction.

As the darkness started closing in, Sepp pressed on. Once again he had to make a choice about whether or not to cross the Norton Sound. Once again, he thought about the number of lives that would be saved by getting back to Nome a day earlier, and he took the risk. He was extremely relieved when he finally reached the other side, and he took a much-needed rest stop. When he woke up a few hours later, he looked back over the Norton Sound where he had just come, and saw that the trail was no longer there! During the night, the storm had broken up the ice and sent it drifting out to sea.

As the blinding, deafening blizzard increased, Sepp and his dogs faced headwinds of up to sixty-five miles per hour – nearly as strong as a hurricane. The next part of the trail had steep mountain ridges and climbed a total of 5,000 feet. The team was so exhausted that they began to stumble as they climbed, but finally, just after reaching the peak, they arrived at the meeting point so they could pass off the serum to the next musher. Fifteen hours later, the serum arrived in Nome, and the town was saved.

Of the twenty different sled dog teams that participated in the serum run, nineteen of them averaged about thirty miles each before passing

the serum off to the next team. Sepp and his dog team led by Togo, however, went a total of 261 miles from the time he raced out of Nome, got the serum from another team, and traveled ninety-one miles back to pass it off to the next musher. The miles that Sepp covered were some of the most dangerous and difficult of the entire run. Through it all, Togo took the lead, staying on the trail, avoiding countless dangers, and keeping the exhausted team moving forward through the fierce blizzard.

Togo was twelve years old when he led his team on the Serum Run, which is old for a sled dog. He never raced again. But if it weren't for Togo, the trouble-maker that turned into a leader, thousands of men, women, and children in Nome would probably have lost their lives.

| | |
|---|---|
| Oglala | Ō glä lä |
| Lakota | Lä kō tä |
| ancestry | an ces²̆ try⁴ |
| assume | as sūm<u>e</u> |
| humbles | hum bl<u>e</u>s² |
| interrelated | in <u>ter</u> rē lā <u>ted</u> |
| prejudice | prej ū dic<u>e</u>² |
| significantly | sig nif i cant ly⁴ |
| collision | cōl li <u>si</u>on² |
| possess | pōs² sess² |
| choreograph | <u>chor</u>² ē ō grap<u>h</u> |
| achieve | ā <u>chieve</u> |
| capabilities | cā pā bil i t<u>ie³s</u>² |
| cooperatives | cō ŏp <u>er</u> ā tiv<u>e</u>s² |

# Billy Mills:
## Running Strong

**B**illy Mills was born in 1938 on the Pine Ridge Indian Reservation in South Dakota. His father was an Oglala Lakota and his mother had both Lakota and white settlers in her ancestry. Billy was the seventh of eight children in the family. As Billy was growing up, he felt particularly close to his father, who taught him things like fishing, hunting, and the values of being a Lakota warrior. Billy remembers, "I was constantly told and challenged to live my life as a warrior. As a warrior, you assume responsibility for yourself. The warrior humbles himself. And the warrior learns the power of giving." The concept of community is another important value of the Lakota. They believe that all people are interrelated and that they all need one another.

Life was challenging for Billy as he grew up. Although the Lakota taught him great values and gave him a strong sense of community, poverty and unemployment were widespread at Pine Ridge, and his family struggled to make ends meet. Just before Billy's eighth birthday, his mother passed away. Later, when he was twelve, his father also died, leaving Billy to be raised by his older siblings. He was also teased by his peers at the reservation because he wasn't one hundred percent Lakota.

Billy found joy and relief in running, which he did often. He loved running through the badlands and canyons on the reservation. Running made him feel strong. In high school he competed in cross country running and track, and he did so well that he earned a scholarship at the University of Kansas.

Attending university was a big step for Billy, since it was his first time entering the "white world." Although he continued to be extremely successful as a runner, he experienced a great deal of prejudice and discrimination. He didn't feel like he fit in at the university, but he also no longer felt like he fit in back at the reservation. In trying to straddle two worlds, he became extremely frustrated. One day during his junior year when he was at his lowest point, he remembered what his father used to say to him: "You have to look deeper, way below the anger, the hurt, the hate, the jealousy, the self-pity, way down deeper where the dreams lie, Son. Find your dream. It's the pursuit of a dream that heals you."

Right then and there, he knew what his dream was: to win a gold medal in the Olympics.

After he finished his degree at the University of Kansas in 1962, Billy joined the U.S. Marines. There he trained as part of the Marine track team, and qualified to run in the 1964 Olympics. He was not considered likely to win the gold medal or even another medal, since his qualifying time was significantly slower than the fastest athletes.

In the Olympics, Billy raced the 10,000 meters, twenty-five laps around the track. During the race, he ran just behind the leaders. In the last lap, Billy was shoved aside by another runner. He fell behind by several meters. Billy quickly moved to an outside lane, sprinted past the others, and finished first, breaking the world record time. His victory, as a practically "unknown" runner who recovered from the collision near the end of the race to go on to win a record-breaking gold, has been called one of the greatest Olympic upsets of all time. No American has won an Olympic gold medal in the 10,000 meters since. Although it was obviously thrilling to Billy to achieve his

"The daily decisions you make in life, not the talent you possess, are what choreograph your destiny."

- Billy Mills

Billy Mills winning the 10,000 meter in the 1964 Olympics
U.S. Marine Corps Photo

dream of winning an Olympic gold medal, he saw a much bigger perspective than simply winning a race. "The ultimate is not to win," he said, "but to reach within the depths of your capabilities and to compete against yourself to the greatest extent possible. When you do that, you have dignity. You have pride. You can walk about with character and pride no matter in what place you happen to finish."

Since that time, Billy has taken seriously the Lakota tradition of making a "giveaway" – that is, giving back to the community that empowered him to achieve his success. He co-founded an organization called "Running Strong for American Indian Youth," which has started and supported all sorts of youth and community programs such as healthcare, housing projects, gardening cooperatives, and building wells. Billy's

"It is the pursuit of excellence that takes you to victory. When you find that passion, it allows you to focus."

– Billy Mills

goal is to empower all Native Americans by helping them have greater stability, promoting healthy attitudes and lifestyles, and inspiring them to value their identity. Because of his commitment to the values he learned as a child, his life has made an enormous impact on generations of children that have come after him.

# Unit 28

| | |
|---|---|
| sepak | sep ak |
| takraw | tā kr<u>aw</u> |
| lunging | lun g<u>ing</u>² |
| stadium | stā di um³ |
| gymnastics | gy̆m² nas tics |
| martial arts | m<u>ar</u> t<u>iä</u>l <u>ar</u>ts |
| agility | ā gil² i ty⁴ |
| circumference | c<u>ir</u>² cum f<u>er</u> enc<u>e</u>² |
| synthetic | sy̆n <u>th</u>et ic |
| badminton | bad min ton |
| Malaysia | Mä l<u>ay</u> s<u>i</u>ä² |
| Philippines | <u>Ph</u>il ip pin<u>e</u>s⁴ ² |
| cooperatively | cō ŏp <u>er</u> ā tiv<u>e</u> ly⁴ |
| renowned | rē n<u>ow</u>n<u>e</u>d² |

# Sepak Takraw

Pal2iyawit / Shutterstock.com

*She watches the small plastic ball bounce off her opponent's head and soar back over the net. In an instant, she leaps up, turns upside-down, spikes the ball with the side of her foot, finishes her mid-air flip, and lands on her feet again. As the ball slams down over the net, the opponent's lunging attempt to kick the ball fails. The stadium explodes with the roaring cheers of fans. With a scream of joy she realizes that her team has just won the King's Cup! They are the best women's sepak takraw team in the world!*

Sepak takraw combines elements of soccer, volleyball, gymnastics, and martial arts. Like soccer, players are not allowed to touch the ball with their hands or arms. Like volleyball, players must keep the ball from touching the ground and get it over a fairly high net to the other side. Like gymnastics, players must have incredible flexibility and agility. And like martial arts, each kick must be precisely executed.

With a circumference of 43 centimeters, a sepak takraw ball is slightly bigger than a softball. It is

Sepak Takraw ball

traditionally made from woven rattan, although modern balls are often made with synthetic fibers instead. The net (which is 1.52 meters high) and court (which is 6.1 meters by 13.4 meters) are about the same size as a badminton net and court.

Each team has three players, and when they receive the ball they must work together to pass the ball over the net without letting it touch the ground. The ball may not be hit more than three times on each side. A match is won by winning the best of five sets. Each set is won by the first team to earn fifteen points.

Most of the time players use their feet to hit the ball, but they can also use their knees, shoulders, or even their heads. It is a challenging game, and players often pull off incredible acrobatic moves to

Pal2iyawit / Shutterstock.com

reach the ball, sometimes sending the ball traveling over 120 kilometers per hour!

The diversity of people and cultures practicing the game has resulted in the development of a variety of styles and creative moves with names like the "Horse-kick," the "Sunback Spike," and the "Cartwheel Serve."

The birth of sepak takraw took place perhaps as far back as a thousand years ago in Southeast Asia. It quickly became popular in places like Malaysia, Thailand, and the Philippines. At first, players just stood in a circle and passed the ball around with their feet, working cooperatively to keep it in the air as long as possible without using their hands, sometimes demonstrating tricks as they did so.

Over time, however, the game developed more and more complexity. The first rules for modern sepak takraw developed in Thailand in the early 1800s, along with the use of a net and the first public competitions. Formal international rules were introduced in the mid 1900s and since then it has spread all around the world.

The process of making sepak takraw an internationally accepted game and making a standardized set of rules also required agreeing on a name. The game was called so many different things in different countries that this was not an easy task. In the end, the international group of organizers compromised with the name "sepak takraw," which is a combination of the Malay word "sepak,"

Pal2iyawit / Shutterstock.com

Pal2iyawit / Shutterstock.com

meaning "kick," and the Thai word "takraw," meaning "woven ball." So, "sepak takraw" literally means "kick ball."

Although Southeast Asia remains the center of sepak takraw's popularity, where it is part of the national school curriculum in some countries, the game has become popular all over the world from Europe to South America. Today over thirty-two countries have organized sepak takraw teams, and many of them compete in worldwide competitions such as the renowned King's Cup World Championship in Thailand and the Asian Games.

| | |
|---|---|
| Louis | Lou³ is |
| prolific | prō lif ic |
| eccentric | ec cen² tric |
| dictated | dic tā t<u>ed</u> |
| dismaying | dis m<u>ay</u> <u>in</u>g |
| episodes | ep i sōd<u>e</u>s² |
| Pacific | Pā cif² ic |
| treasure | tr<u>ea</u>s²² ūr<u>e</u> |
| Jekyll | Jek y̆ll |
| pleasantest | pl<u>ea</u>s²² ant est |
| arrant | ar rant |
| leaden | l<u>ea</u>d² en |
| abroad | ā br<u>oa</u>d^x |
| curious | cū ri³ <u>ou</u>s⁴ |

# Robert Louis Stevenson

Robert Louis Stevenson was a prolific writer of short stories, novels, travel essays, poems, and even musical compositions. As a child, however, he did not appear to have a great future. Stevenson was born in Scotland in 1850. He was constantly sick. His health often kept him from being able to go to school, so he spent a lot of time at home being cared for by his nanny. The poems that follow are from a book of poems called *A Child's Garden of Verses*, which he dedicated to this nanny.

When he was healthy enough to go to school, he was considered strange and eccentric and did not fit in well with the other students. He also did not learn to read until later than most of the other students. He always loved telling stories, though, and he often dictated his stories to his nanny or his mother before he learned to write.

Robert Louis Stevenson

Stevenson came from a long line of famous lighthouse engineers, and at first he studied engineering as well. When he was twenty years old, however, Stevenson decided that he wanted to be a writer instead of an engineer, which must have been somewhat dismaying to his family.

As an adult, Stevenson continued to have episodes of very poor health, and at his doctor's advice, he spent more and more time in warmer climates, such as the south of France. He continued to travel a great deal throughout his lifetime, and many of his books reflected those experiences. Some of his most beloved books include the pirate tale *Treasure Island*, the classic adventure story *Kidnapped*, and *The Strange Case of Dr. Jekyll and Mr. Hyde*. Stevenson eventually ended up living in the South Pacific, where he died in 1894.

# The Swing

How do you like to go up in a swing,
    Up in the air so blue?
Oh, I do think it the pleasantest thing
    Ever a child can do!

Up in the air and over the wall,
    Till I can see so wide,
Rivers and trees and cattle and all
    Over the countryside–

Till I look down on the garden green,
    Down on the roof so brown–
Up in the air I go flying again,
    Up in the air and down!

# My Shadow

I have a little shadow that
    goes in and out with me,
And what can be the use of him
    is more than I can see.
He is very, very like me
    from the heels up to the head;
And I see him jump before me,
    when I jump into my bed.

The funniest thing about him
    is the way he likes to grow—
Not at all like proper children,
    which is always very slow;
For he sometimes shoots up taller
    like an india-rubber ball,
And he sometimes gets so little
    that there's none of him at all.

He hasn't got a **notion** of
    how children ought to play,
And can only make a fool of me
    in every sort of way.
He stays so close beside me,
    he's a coward, you can see;
I'd think shame to stick to nursie
    as that shadow sticks to me!

One morning, very early,
    before the sun was up,
I rose and found the shining dew
    on every buttercup;
But my lazy little shadow,
    like an **arrant** sleepy-head,
Had stayed at home behind me
    and was fast asleep in bed.

# The Land of Counterpane

When I was sick and lay a-bed,
I had two pillows at my head,
And all my toys beside me lay
To keep me happy all the day.

And sometimes for an hour or so
I watched my leaden soldiers go,
With different uniforms and drills,
Among the bed-clothes, through the hills.

And sometimes sent my ships in fleets
All up and down among the sheets;
Or brought my trees and houses out,
And planted cities all about.

I was the giant great and still
That sits upon the pillow-hill,
And sees before him, **dale** and plain,
The pleasant Land of **Counterpane**.

# The Land of Nod

From breakfast on through all the day
At home among my friends I stay,
But every night I go **abroad**
Afar into the land of Nod.

All by myself I have to go,
With none to tell me what to do—
All alone beside the streams
And up the mountain-sides of dreams.

The strangest things are there for me,
Both things to eat and things to see,
And many frightening sights abroad
Till morning in the land of Nod.

Try as I like to find the way,
I never can get back by day,
Nor can remember plain and clear
The curious music that I hear.

# Unit 30

| | |
|---|---|
| torrential | <u>tor</u> ren <u>tial</u> |
| esteemed | es t<u>ee</u>m<u>ed</u>² |
| renowned | rē n<u>own</u><u>ed</u>² |
| patients | pā <u>tie</u>nts |
| fluently | flū ent l̄y⁴ |
| contagious | con tā <u>giou</u>s⁴ |
| epidemic | ep i dem ic |
| frugal | frū gal |
| generosity | gen² <u>er</u> os i ty⁴ |
| vulnerable | vul n<u>er</u> ā bl<u>e</u> |
| philanthropist | <u>phil</u> an <u>thr</u>ō pist |
| amassed | ā mass<u>ed</u>³ |
| abundance | ā bun danc<u>e</u>² |

# Biddy Mason

Biddy Mason was born as a slave in 1818. When she was eighteen years old, she was given as a wedding present to Robert and Rebecca Smith, who lived in Mississippi. Biddy's younger sister Hannah was also a slave for the Smith family. While they were in Mississippi, Biddy gave birth to three daughters.

In 1848, Robert Smith decided to take his family and all their slaves, including Biddy and her children, and move west. They joined a caravan of wagons in March and began traveling across the country for nearly seven months and two thousand miles.

Along the way, they encountered torrential rains, areas with little for their livestock to eat, wolf attacks, and a snowstorm. As they traveled, it was Biddy's job to walk behind the ox-drawn wagon and herd the cattle. She also prepared meals, took care of the six Smith children, nursed anyone who was sick or injured, and helped deliver babies. Her own three daughters were ages ten, four, and an infant that she carried on her back.

The Smith household first settled in Utah,

but three years later they moved farther to San Bernadino, California. The state of California did not allow slavery, so Robert Smith tried to keep it secret that he had slaves. After a few years, however, he began to get nervous that his slaves would be taken from him, so he decided to move to Texas, where slavery was still legal.

Biddy and her family had made friends with a number of free African Americans in California. One of the free families they had gotten to know was the esteemed Owens family, who lived in nearby Los Angeles. Biddy's oldest daughter, Ellen, who was now seventeen years old, had fallen in love with Charles Owens. Charles' father, Robert Owens, was a successful cowboy and businessman who was also friends with the local sheriff.

When Biddy overheard her owner's plans to take them all to Texas, she quietly informed Charles. Since Biddy's sister, Hannah, who was also owned by Robert Smith, was about to give birth to her eighth child, the family was unable to leave immediately. But Robert Smith suspected that Biddy might be making plans to escape, so he took everyone to camp out in the mountains until Hannah's baby was born. That is when the Owens family made their move. Together with the sheriff, they organized a group of cowboys to ride into the camp and rescue Biddy and her family.

Biddy Mason
Public Domain

Biddy's friends then helped her bring her case to court. They decided that the local jail would be the best place to keep Biddy and her family safe until the court case was finished. During the trial, Robert Smith threatened Biddy and her family, tried to bribe Biddy's lawyer to drop the case, and attempted to kidnap some of the children. However, the judge sided with Biddy and granted her and her whole family freedom.

Biddy was thirty-seven years old when she won her freedom. She and her family moved to Los Angeles (which was a small town of about 1,600 people at the time), where the Owens family invited her to stay with them.

Biddy found a job as a nurse and midwife under a respected doctor. Soon her skills were **renowned** and her services were in high demand. She treated all the patients that came to her, regardless of their race or whether or not they could pay. Since many of her patients spoke Spanish, she even learned to speak Spanish fluently. She nursed hospital patients

> "If you hold your hand closed, nothing good can come in. But the open hand is blessed, for it gives in abundance, even as it receives."
>
> Biddy Mason

and prisoners, and risked her life to help highly-contagious smallpox victims during an epidemic. Biddy was a hard worker, but she was also very frugal. She saved her earnings carefully. In 1866 she bought her first piece of property. She became an excellent businesswoman, continuing to buy and sell property, which increased significantly in value as it became part of the quickly growing downtown Los Angeles.

As Biddy's wealth grew, so did her generosity. Her house became well-known as a refuge for newcomers and anyone that needed assistance. She helped feed and shelter poor and vulnerable people of all races, helped **found** an elementary school for black children, and with her son-in-law, Charles Owens, started the first black church in Los Angeles. When a flood in 1884 destroyed many homes and farms in the area, crowds of people were homeless and threatened with starvation. Biddy immediately donated a large amount of money to a local store to provide free food and supplies to the homeless families.

By the time Biddy Mason passed away in 1891, she had become famous as a skilled midwife and nurse, a wealthy landowner, and a compassionate **philanthropist**. She had amassed nearly $300,000 in investments, which would be worth over $8 million today. Her legacy continued as her children and grandchildren followed in her footsteps by becoming strong leaders in the community as well.

# Appendix A:
# Phonograms and Spelling Rules

A list of the new phonograms and spelling rules needed for each unit

| | Phonograms | | Spelling Rules |
|---|---|---|---|
| **1** | a-z | 11 | Q always needs a U; therefore, U is not a vowel here. |
| | | 21 | To make a noun plural, add the ending -S; unless the word hisses or changes, then add -ES. Some nouns have no change or an irregular spelling. |
| **2** | ck ee ng th | 26 | CK is used only after a single vowel which says its short sound. |
| | | 29 | Z, never S, spells /z/ at the beginning of a base word. |
| **3** | er or ea sh | 18 | SH spells /sh/ at the beginning of a base word and at the end of the syllable. SH never spells /sh/ at the beginning of any syllable after the first one, except for the ending -ship. |
| | | 4 | A E O U usually say their long sounds at the end of a syllable. |
| **4** | oi oy es | 3 | English words do not end in I, U, V, or J. |
| | | 31.1 | Any vowel may say one of the schwa sounds, /ŭ/ or /ĭ/, in an unstressed syllable or unstressed word. |
| **5** | ai ay | 9 | AY usually spells the sound /ā/ at the end of a base word. |
| | | 10 | When a word ends with the phonogram A, it says /ä/. |
| **6** | ar ch oo | 30 | We often double F, L, and S after a single, short or broad vowel at the end of a base word. Occasionally other letters also are doubled. |
| **7** | oa oe | 31.2 | O may say /ŭ/ in a stressed syllable next to W, TH, M, N, or V. |
| **8** | igh wh | 28 | Phonograms ending in GH are used only at the end of a base word or before the letter T. The GH is either silent or pronounced /f/. |
| | | 31.3 | AR and OR may say their schwa sound, /er/, in an unstressed syllable. |

| | Phonograms | | Spelling Rules |
|---|---|---|---|
| **9** | au<br>aw<br>augh | 5 | I and Y may say /ĭ/or /ī/ at the end of a syllable. |
| **10** | ou<br>ow<br>ough | 22 | To make a verb 3rd person singular, add the ending -S; unless the word hisses or changes, then add -ES. Only four verbs are irregular. |
| | | 24 | -FUL is a suffix written with one L when added to another syllable. |
| **11** | tch | 27 | TCH is used only after a single vowel which says its short or broad sound. |
| **12** | kn<br>gn | 8 | I and O may say /ī/and /ō/ when followed by two consonants. |
| **13** | ir<br>ur<br>ear | | |
| **14** | ed<br>ew | 19 | To make a verb past tense, add the ending -ED unless it is an irregular verb. |
| | | 20 | -ED, past tense ending, forms another syllable when the base word ends in /d/ or /t/. Otherwise, -ED says /d/ or /t/. |
| **15** | ui | 1 | C always softens to /s/ when followed by E, I, or Y. Otherwise, C says /k/. |
| | | 2 | G may soften to /j/ only when followed by E, I, or Y. Otherwise, G says /g/. |
| **16** | wr | 12.1 | The vowel says its long sound because of the E. |
| | | 13 | Drop the silent final E when adding a vowel suffix only if it is allowed by other spelling rules. |
| **17** | wor<br>ay | 12.2 | English words do not end in V or U. |
| | | 12.3 | The C says /s/ and the G says /j/ because of the E. |
| **18** | ph | 12.4 | Every syllable must have a written vowel. |
| | | 12.5 | Add an E to keep singular words that end in the letter S from looking plural. |
| **19** | ei<br>ey<br>eigh | 12.6 | Add an E to make the word look bigger. |
| | | 12.7 | TH says its voiced sound /TH/ because of the E. |

| | Phonograms | | Spelling Rules |
|---|---|---|---|
| **20** | cei | **12.8** | Add an E to clarify meaning. |
| | | **12.9** | Unseen reason. |
| **21** | bu gu | **6** | When a one-syllable word end in a single vowel Y, it says /ī/. |
| | | **7** | Y says /ē/ only at the end of a multi-syllable word. I says /ē/ at the end of a syllable that is followed by a vowel and at the end of foreign words. |
| | | **15** | Single vowel Y changes to I when adding any ending, unless the ending begins with I. |
| | | **16** | Two I's cannot be next to one another in English words. |
| **22** | ie | | |
| **23** | dge eo | **25** | DGE is used only after a single vowel which says its short sound. |
| **24** | ti ci si eo our | **17** | TI, CI, and SI are used only at the beginning of any syllable after the first one. |
| **25** | gi | **14** | Double the last consonant when adding a vowel suffix to words ending in one vowel followed by one consonant only if the syllable before the suffix is stressed. |
| **26** | eo bt | | |
| **27** | | | |
| **28** | | | |
| **29** | | **23** | AL- is a prefix written with one L when preceding another syllable. |
| **30** | gi | | |

# Appendix B: Sources

All images not otherwise credited
are from Shutterstock.com.

## Buck Got Stuck

**Illustration**

Libby Johnson

## Futnet

The European Futnet Association official website. Accessed September 2013. www.futnet.eu/

Union Internationale de Futnet (UNIF) website. 2011. www.unifut.net/

Wikipedia, s.v. "Futnet." Accessed September 2013. en.wikipedia.org/wiki/Futnet

**Photo sources**

Futnet players, p. 18: European Futnet Association. Accessed September 2013. http://www.futnet.eu/multimedia/photo-gallery/czech-open-prerov/

## Astronauts

National Aeronautics and Space Administration website. Accessed October 2013. www.nasa.gov

Nelson, Maria. *Life on the International Space Station.* New York: Gareth Stevens Publishing, 2013.

Parker, Steve, and Alex Pang. *Space Exploration.* Broomall, Pa.: Mason Crest Publishers, 2011.

**Photo sources**

Astronaut floating, p. 26: NASA. February 11, 1984. Image # S84-27011. grin.hq.nasa.gov/ABSTRACTS/GPN-2000-001156.html

Astronauts and floating food, p. 27: NASA. www.nasa.gov/audience/formedia/presskits/spacefood/gallery_iss005e16336.html

## Molasses Banana Bread

"Grandma's Molasses Banana Bread." Cooks.com. Accessed October 2013. www.cooks.com/recipe/ih0119xh/grandmas-molasses-banana-bread. html

"Molasses Banana Bread." Allrecipes. Accessed October 2013. http:// allrecipes.com/recipe/17281/molasses-banana-bread/

"Molasses Banana Bread." Cooks.com. Accessed October 2013. www.cooks. com/recipe/wp35l8ue/molasses-banana-bread.html


## Stars of the Sea

Blaxland, Beth. *Sea Stars, Sea Urchins, and Their Relatives: Echinoderms.* Philadelphia: Chelsea House Publishers, 2003.

**Photo sources**

Starfish arm detail, p. 36: Picard, André-Philipe D. "Détail bras d'étoile de mer.jpg." Wikipedia. 13 September 2011. http://en.wikipedia.org/wiki/ File:D%C3%A9tail_bras_d%27%C3%A9toile_de_mer.jpg.


## The Toothpick Fighters

Hearn, Lafcadio. *Chin Chin Kobakama. Japanese Fairy Tale Series, No. 25.* Tokyo: T. Hasegawa, 1903. Internet Archive. Accessed November 2013. https://archive.org/details/chinchinkobakama00hearrich

Sakade, Florence. "The Toothpick Warriors." *Peach Boy and Other Japanese Children's Favorite Stories.* Rutland, VT: Tuttle, 1984.

**Illustrations**

Libby Johnson


## William Kamkwamba

Kamkwamba, William, and Bryan Mealer. *The Boy Who Harnessed the Wind: Creating Currents of Electricity and Hope.* New York, NY: William Morrow, 2009.

McCann, Michelle Rohm and David Hahn. *Boys Who Rocked the World: Heroes from King Tut to Bruce Lee.* New York: Aladdin/Beyond Words, 2012.

Wikipedia, s.v. "William Kamkwamba." Accessed December 2013. https://en.wikipedia.org/wiki/William_Kamkwamba

**Photo sources**

Windmill, p. 48: Tom Rielly. Shared on flickr by Erik (HASH) Hersman. www.flickr.com/photos/18288598@N00/622366993/. Reproduced under a Creative Commons license.

William Kamkwamba TED talk, p. 49: Erik (HASH) Hersman. June 6, 2007. www.flickr.com/photos/18288598@N00/532927602/. Reproduced under a Creative Commons license.


## Geothermal Energy

Altman, Linda Jacobs. *Letting Off Steam: The Story of Geothermal Energy.* Minneapolis: Carolrhoda Books, 1989.

Graham, Ian. Geothermal and Bio-Energy. Energy Forever? Austin, TX: Raintree Steck-Vaughn, 1999.

Sherman, Josepha. *Geothermal Power.* Mankato, Minn.: Capstone Press, 2004.

White, Nancy. *Using Earth's Underground Heat.* New York: Bearport, 2010.

Wikipedia, s.v. "Geothermal energy." Accessed December 2013. https://en.wikipedia.org/wiki/Geothermal_energy


## The Tale of Paul Bunyan

McCormick, Dell J. *Paul Bunyan Swings His Axe.* Caldwell, Idaho: Caxton, 1987.

"Paul Bunyan." American Folklore. Accessed January 2014. http://americanfolklore.net/folklore/paul-bunyan/

Schlosser, S.E. "Babe the Blue Ox" *Minnesota Tall Tales.* American Folklore. Accessed January 2014. http://americanfolklore.net/folklore/2010/07/babe_the_blue_ox.html

Schlosser, S.E. "Birth of Paul Bunyan" *Maine Tall Tales.* American Folklore. Accessed January 2014. http://americanfolklore.net/folklore/2010/07/the_birth_of_paul_bunyan.html

Wikipedia, s.v. "Paul Bunyan." Accessed January 2014 https://en.wikipedia.org/wiki/Paul_Bunyan

**Photo sources**

Lumberjacks, p. 60: Kerry and Co, Sydney, Australia. Tyrrell Photographic Collection. www.powerhousemuseum.com/collection/database/?irn=29300


## The Story of Chocolate

Burleigh, Robert. *Chocolate: Riches from the Rainforest.* New York: Abrams, 2002.

Stewart, Melissa and Allen Young. *No Monkeys, No Chocolate.* Watertown, MA: Charlesbridge, 2013.

Wikipedia, s.v. "Chocolate." Accessed January 2014. https://en.wikipedia.org/wiki/Chocolate

Woods, Samuel G. *Chocolate From Start to Finish.* Made in the U.S.A. series. Woodbridge, CT: Blackbirch Press, 1999.

**Photo sources**

Mayan Chocolate image, p. 67: Wikipedia. Public domain. en.wikipedia.org/wiki/File:Mayan_people_and_chocolate.jpg


## A Perilous Escape / Robert Smalls

Westwood, Howard. "Robert Smalls: Commander of the Planter During the American Civil War." HistoryNet. 2006. Originally published in *Civil War Times*, May 1986. Accessed February 2014. http://www.historynet.com/robert-smalls-commander-of-the-planter-during-the-american-civil-war.htm

"Who Was Congressman Robert Smalls?" The Life and Times of Congressman Robert Smalls: A Traveling Exhibition. Accessed February 2014. http://www.robertsmalls.com/history2.html

Halfmann, Janet, and Duane Smith. *Seven Miles to Freedom: The Robert Smalls Story.* New York: Lee & Low Books, 2008.

Altman, Susan. *Extraordinary African-Americans.* Rev. ed. New York: Children's Press, 2001.

Cooper, Michael L. *From Slave to Civil War Hero: The Life and Times of Robert Smalls.* New York: Lodestar Books, 1994.

Kranz, Rachel, and Philip Koslow. Biographical Dictionary of African Americans. Rev. ed. New York: Facts on File, 1999.

**Photo sources**

Planter, p. 74: "Gunboat Planter." *Harper's Weekly*, June 14, 1862, p. 372. Wikipedia. Updated 13 February 2014. https://commons.wikimedia. org/wiki/File:Gunboat_Planter.png

Fort Sumter, p. 77: "Fort Sumter 1860." Public Domain. Wikipedia. Accessed February 2014. https://en.wikipedia.org/wiki/ File:FortSumter1860.jpg

Clipper ship, p. 78: "Clipper Ship Southern Cross Leaving Boston Harbor." 1851. Public Domain. Accessed February 2014. http://en.wikipedia. org/wiki/File:Clipper_Ship_Southern_Cross_Leaving_Boston_ Harbor_1851.jpeg

Slaves working, p. 81: "James Hopkinsons Plantation Slaves Planting Sweet Potatoes.jpg." Wikipedia. Updated 23 March 2013. Public Domain. http://en.wikipedia.org/wiki/File:James_Hopkinsons_Plantation_ Slaves_Planting_Sweet_Potatoes.jpg

Charleston, p. 82: "Last palmetto Charleston 1865.jpg." Wikipedia. Updated 3 April 2010. Public Domain. http://en.wikipedia.org/wiki/File:Last_ palmetto_Charleston_1865.jpg

Planter, p. 83: "NH 74054 Steamer Planter.jpg." Wikipedia. Updated 23 December 2008. Public Domain. http://en.wikipedia.org/wiki/ File:NH_74054_Steamer_Planter.jpg

Robert Smalls, p. 84: Library of Congress. Brady-Handy Photograph Collection. Accessed February 2014. http://www.loc.gov/pictures/item/ brh2003000291/PP/. Call number: LC-BH826-825

House of Robert Smalls, p. 85: "Robert Smalls house (Beaufort, South Carolina).jpg." Wikipedia. Updated 22 March 2008. Public Domain. http://en.wikipedia.org/wiki/File:Robert_Smalls_House_%28Beaufort,_ South_Carolina%29.jpg

## Banyan Trees

Bash, Barbara. *In the Heart of the Village: The World of the Indian Banyan Tree.* San Francisco: Sierra Club Books, 1996.

Wikipedia, s.v. "Banyan." Accessed March 2014. http://en.wikipedia.org/wiki/Banyan

"Ficus benghalensis (banyan)." Kew Royal Botanic Gardens. Accessed March 2014. http://www.kew.org/science-conservation/plants-fungi/ficus-benghalensis-banyan

### Photo sources

Swinging girl, p. 96: Bures, Stephen. "SIEM REAP, CAMBODIA- APRIL 1: Unidentified child plays in jungle at Ta Prohm Temple." Shutterstock. com. Image ID:81419668.


## The Boy Who Wanted a Drum

"A Drum." Ramanujan, A.K., ed. *Folktales from India: A Selection of Oral Tales from Twenty-Two Languages.* NY: Pantheon, 1991.

Nanji, Shenaz. "The Drummer Boy." *Indian Tales: A Barefoot Collection.* Cambridge, MA: Barefoot Books, 2007.


## The Message of the Drum

"Drums and Drumming Language across West Africa." Linear Population Model (blog). June 25, 2011. linearpopulationmodel.blogspot. com/2011/06/drums-and-drumming-language-across-west.html

Gleick, James. *The Information: a History, a Theory, a Flood.* New York: Pantheon Books, 2011.

Wikipedia, s.v. "Drums in communication." Accessed April 2014. en.wikipedia.org/wiki/Drums_in_communication

Wikipedia, s.v. "Slit drum." Accessed April 2014. en.wikipedia.org/wiki/Slit_gong

### Photo sources

Woman drumming, p. 111: photo courtesy of Samaan Frajallah.

Talking drum, p. 112: Wikimedia Commons. Last updated 3 March 2015. http://en.wikipedia.org/wiki/File:TalkingDrum.jpg

Bamileke Tamtam, p. 113: Wikimedia Commons. Last updated 29 December 2005. http://en.wikipedia.org/wiki/File:TamTam.jpg

Drummers, p. 114: Davis, Paula. 2004. Last updated June 24, 2006. http://en.wikipedia.org/wiki/File:Kwarastatedrummers.jpg. Reproduced under a Creative Commons license.

## Grace Murray Hopper: Computer Pioneer

Chin-Lee, Cynthia. *Amelia to Zora - Twenty-Six Women Who Changed the World.* Watertown, MA: Charlesbridge, 2005.

Vare, Ethlie A. and Greg Ptacek. *Women Inventors & Their Discoveries.* Minneapolis: Oliver Press, 1993.

Epstein, Vivian Sheldon. *History of Women in Science for Young People.* Denver, Colo.: VSE Publisher, 1994.

Wikipedia, s.v. "Grace Hopper." Accessed March 2014. https://en.wikipedia.org/wiki/Grace_Hopper

Dickason, Elizabeth. "Remembering Grace Murray Hopper - A Legend in Her Own Time." About.com. Accessed March 2014. http://inventors.about.com/od/hstartinventors/a/Grace_Hopper.htm

Danis, Sharron Ann. "Rear Admiral Grace Murray Hopper." Updated Feb. 16, 1997. ei.cs.vt.edu/~history/Hopper.Danis.html

**Photo sources**

Mark I, p. 119: "Harvard Mark I Computer - Right Segment.JPG." Wikimedia Commons. Last updated 26 February 2006. https://commons.wikimedia.org/wiki/File:Harvard_Mark_I_Computer_-_Right_Segment.JPG

Bug in log book, p. 120: "H96566k.jpg." 9 Sept. 1947. US Naval Historical Center. Public Domain. Wikimedia Commons. Last updated July 21, 2012. https://commons.wikimedia.org/wiki/File:H96566k.jpg

Grace Murray Hopper and UNIVAC, p. 121: "Grace Hopper and UNIVAC.jpg." Wikimedia Commons. Last updated June 4, 2012. https://commons.wikimedia.org/wiki/File:Grace_Hopper_and_UNIVAC.jpg

Grace Murray Hopper, p. 122: U.S. Navy photo. 20 January 1984. Public Domain. Wikimedia Commons. Last updated 23 Dec. 2010. http://en.wikipedia.org/wiki/File:Commodore_Grace_M._Hopper,_USN_%28covered%29.jpg

U.S.S. Hopper, p. 123: U.S. Navy. "US Navy 110415-N-KT462-199 The guided-missile destroyer USS Hopper." Public Domain. Wikimedia Commons. Last updated 15 April 2011. https://en.wikipedia.org/wiki/USS_Hopper#/media/File:Flickr_-_Official_U.S._Navy_Imagery_-_USS_Hopper_leaves_Joint_Base_Pearl_Harbor-Hickam..jpg

## Iditarod

"Iditarod Questions and Answers." Don Bowers' 2000 Musher Diary. Accessed May 2014. www.nanuq.net/donbowers/pageq&a.htm

Iditarod website. Iditarod Trail Committee. Accessed May 2014. iditarod.com

Bowers, Donald Jr. "Shaktoolik to Koyuk." Iditarod website. Iditarod Trail Committee. Accessed May 2014. iditarod.com/about/the-iditarod-trail/shaktoolik-to-koyuk/

Sherwonit, Bill, and Jeff Schultz. *Iditarod: The Great Race to Nome*. Bothell, WA: Alaska Northwest Books, 1991.
The quote in the final paragraph of "Iditarod: The Greatest Race on Earth" is from Joe Redington, Sr., the "father of the Iditarod," quoted in *Iditarod: The Great Race to Nome*, p. 7.

## Togo

Salisbury, Gay and Laney. *The Cruelest Miles: The Heroic Story of Dogs and Men in a Race Against an Epidemic*. New York: Norton, 2003.

Blake, Robert J. *Togo*. New York: Philomel Books, 2002.

Wikipedia, s.v. "Leonhard Seppala." Accessed May 2014. en.wikipedia.org/wiki/Leonhard_Seppala

Wikipedia, s.v. "1925 serum run to Nome." Accessed May 2014. en.wikipedia.org/wiki/1925_serum_run_to_Nome

## Billy Mills: Running Strong

"Billy Mills." Running Past. Accessed February 2014. www.runningpast. com/billy_mills.htm

"About Billy Mills." Running Strong for American Indian Youth website. Accessed February 2014. indianyouth.org//about-us/about-billy-mills

Wikipedia, s.v. "Billy Mills." Accessed February 2014. en.wikipedia.org/ wiki/Billy_Mills

Moore, Kenny. "Racing Split." Runner's World. February 1, 2012. http:// www.runnersworld.com/runners-stories/racing-split

**Photo sources**

Crossing the finish, p. 150. "BillyMills Crossing Finish Line 1964Olympics. jpg." U.S. Marine Corps. Wikipedia. Marine Corps Photo A411758. Public Domain. Updated 15 August 2008. en.wikipedia.org/wiki/ File:BillyMills_Crossing_Finish_Line_1964Olympics.jpg

## Sepak Takraw

Wikipedia, s.v. "Sepak takraw." Accessed April 2014. en.wikipedia.org/wiki/ Sepak_takraw

Sepak Takraw Official Website. Accessed April 2014. www.sepaktakraw.org

Takraw Guide. Accessed April 2014. takraw.webark.org

## Robert Louis Stevenson

"Life." RLS Website. Accessed April 2014. www.robert-louis-stevenson.org/ life

Wikipedia, s.v. "Robert Louis Stevenson." Accessed April 2014. en.wikipedia.org/wiki/Robert_Louis_Stevenson

"Robert Louis Stevenson Biography." Biography.com. Accessed April 2014. www.biography.com/people/robert-louis-stevenson-9494571#the-writer-emerges&awesm=~oHy7OKp6KHOoTF

Stevenson, Robert Louis. *A Child's Garden of Verses*. Scribner, 1905. Accessed on Project Gutenberg, April 2014. http://www.gutenberg.org/ files/25609/25609-h/25609-h.htm

## Biddy Mason

Wikipedia, s.v. "Biddy Mason." Accessed January 2014. en.wikipedia.org/wiki/Biddy_Mason

"From Slavery to Entrepreneur, Biddy Mason." African American Registry. 2013. www.aaregistry.org/historic_events/view/slavery-entrepreneur-biddy-mason

Colman, Penny. *Adventurous Women: Eight True Stories About Women Who Made a Difference.* New York: Holt, 2006.

Furbee, Mary R. *Outrageous Women of the American Frontier.* New York: J. Wiley, 2002.

Igus, Toyomi. *Great Women In The Struggle: An Introduction for Young Readers.* Book of Black Heroes, Vol. 2. Orange, NJ: Just Us Books, 1991.

### Photo sources

Biddy Mason, p. 169: "Biddy Mason (00026783).jpg." Wikimedia Commons. Last updated 23 July, 2014. Public Domain. https://commons.wikimedia.org/wiki/File:Biddy_Mason_(00026783).jpg